GAY MEN, STRAIGHT JOBS

GAY MEN, STRAIGHT JOBS

BY DAN WOOG

alyson books
los angeles | new york

MANUFACTURED IN THE UNITED STATES OF AMERICA.

THIS TRADE PAPERBACK ORIGINAL IS PUBLISHED BY ALYSON PUBLICATIONS,
P.O. BOX 4371, LOS ANGELES, CALIFORNIA 90078-4371.
DISTRIBUTION IN THE UNITED KINGDOM BY
TURNAROUND PUBLISHER SERVICES LTD.,
UNIT 3, OLYMPIA TRADING ESTATE, COBURG ROAD, WOOD GREEN,
LONDON N22 6TZ ENGLAND.

FIRST EDITION: OCTOBER 2001

01 02 03 04 05 a 10 9 8 7 6 5 4 3 2 1

ISBN 1-55583-616-X

LIBRARY OF CONGRESS CATALOGING-IN-PUBLICATION DATA
WOOG, DAN, 1953–
  GAY MEN, STRAIGHT JOBS / BY DAN WOOG.
  ISBN 155583-616-X
  1. GAY MEN—EMPLOYMENT—UNITED STATES. 2. GAY MEN—BIOGRAPHY.
  3. CLOSETED GAYS—UNITED STATES. 4. PROFESSIONAL EMPLOYEES—UNITED
  STATES. 5. EMPLOYEES—UNITED STATES. I. TITLE.
  HD6285.5.U6 W664 2001
  331.5'3—DC21   2001033544

CREDITS
COVER DESIGN BY MATT SAMS.
COVER PHOTOGRAPHY BY STUDIO 1435.

Contents

Introduction

For many years, work has had as great an effect on how out a gay man is as any other factor, including geography, religion, and family background. It was assumed that in a few professions nearly every man was gay: interior decorating, floristry, ballet. Other jobs, though not "exclusively gay," were thought to attract greater-than-normal percentages of gay men: flight attending, nursing, church organists. (Some would add "priest" to the list, but I hesitate to go there...)

Today, however, most people recognize that gay men are everywhere. We are farmers as well as florists; we fly jumbo jets as well as serve peanuts on them; we are, to paraphrase Willie Nelson, cowboys and doctors and lawyers and such. (Which means, of course, that we are also country music singers.)

But being a gay firefighter, prison guard, railroad worker, criminal defense attorney, or television news reporter is one thing; being *openly* gay at the fire station, prison, rail yard, courthouse, or newsroom is quite another. Consequently, at the dawn of the 21st century, those are exactly the places where the most interesting stories of gay America can be found.

Last year, I set out to discover what it is like to be a gay man working at "heterosexual jobs," as most people—gay as well as straight—would call them. I wanted to learn how being gay affects one's choice of work and one's on-the-job experience. I was curious to learn: How out can people be in "traditionally straight" jobs? How do out workers relate to bosses, colleagues, clients, and customers? Where is the intersection between work life and personal life, and is it different for a gay man than a straight man?

The answers, as I had expected, are all over the lot. Every human being is a unique individual, so every gay man's story is his own. The tale of a gay logger is not the same as that of a gay oil rig worker, cement truck driver, telephone lineman, or judge. Who would expect it to be? (Furthermore, of course, the story of one gay logger is not the same as that of the next gay logger.)

On the other hand, all out gay men—no matter what profession or job—share certain experiences that straight men never can. These experiences revolve around overcoming homophobia, be it subtle or overt, in the workplace. And even though every gay man's story differs, the issues are often the same: When is it appropriate to come out at work? Who do you tell, and how? What about promotions? How do you keep your personal life private—and should you?

Over the course of a year, I interviewed dozens of men about their sexuality and their work. A few, I realized, had no story to tell: They are out on the job, and that is that. But most told intriguing tales. Some of the men I talked with are completely closeted both at work and home. Others are not out, or are semi-out at work and way out at home; for them, every day is a demanding, energy-draining balancing act. Still others are fully out in all facets of their lives; their experiences range from joyful to miserable. For some, being out at work has been easy; for others, coming out on the job remains the most frightening thing they have ever done.

Because they understand the importance of showing America—gay and straight alike—that gay men work in every conceivable field, these men were willing to share their stories. Many wanted their full names used; some asked to be called only by their first names or by aliases. (Aliases appear in quotation marks the first time the alias appears.)

Some of their stories are positive, even liberating; others are negative, even tragic. Taken together, all reveal important truths about what truly makes today's America "work."

Dan Woog
Westport, Conn.
July 2001
www.danwoog.com

"Vinnie Caputo": Firefighter

Like many American boys, "Vinnie Caputo" always wanted to be a fireman. He was fascinated by fire engines and sirens, and was thrilled by the notion of being hailed a hero simply for doing his job. He grew up around the corner from a firehouse in a large Northeastern city and hung out there as a boy. The firemen treated him well and stoked his dream.

But Vinnie had a problem, he thought: He was gay. He had grown up hearing firehouse chatter, in which any snippet of weakness was fair game. If you were getting divorced, the guys ragged on you about your wife's other man. If you went to the doctor for tests, your best friend asked if he could have your locker when you died. And if you bent over in the shower to pick up a bar of soap, the gibes could be merciless.

Vinnie had known he was gay for as long as he had known he wanted to be a fireman: forever. As the child of divorced parents, a poor student, and a loner who did not play sports, becoming a fireman was the best way he knew to make something of his life. He promised himself he would never do anything to destroy that chance. And once he got his opportunity—after scoring well on a battery of tests, undergoing rigorous training, immersing himself in the fire department's history and traditions, and vowing to sacrifice his life for his colleagues, just as they would for him—Vinnie understood that coming out in the firehouse would be an enormous mistake, almost a desecration of the department he loves.

Which is why Vinnie Caputo lives in two separate worlds. During his 24-hour work shifts he is a straight-talking, straight-acting, straight-appearing fireman who shares virtually no details of his private life with the men he calls his "brothers" and with whom he shares sleeping quarters and constant conversation. Off duty, he is a gay man with a slowly growing circle of gay friends who, like Vinnie, enjoy bicycling, running, hiking, and snowboarding. A few of them know what Vinnie does for a living. Most do not. He remains petrified that somehow the news will leak: *Vinnie Caputo is a gay firefighter.* That, he believes, could mean the end of his career—and the life he adores.

"At work now, I'm respected. I'm part of a majority," he explains, his voice strong with the conviction of a man who has analyzed a problem from many angles and is convinced his solution is the most appropriate one. "I'm really afraid that if I was out, I'd be part of a tiny, almost nonexistent, minority. I know, at best, I'd be isolated. Probably there'd be a lot of verbal torture. I'm not afraid of physical harm—that doesn't happen here—but I can't let these guys know me. It's hard just talking about fire department stuff all the time, but that's the way it has to be. That's just the way it is in this job."

Firehouse life is unique. Living space is tight, centered around a communal kitchen. Vinnie compares it to a dormitory. Working, training, maintaining equipment, cooking, eating, and sleeping side by side, 24 hours at a clip, the men of a firehouse (and, even at the dawn of the 21st century, firefighters are almost all male) develop bonds unmatched in perhaps any other profession. The department's camaraderie extends far beyond each 24-hour shift. "If a guy needs help putting a roof on his house," Vinnie says, "you go out and help him put on the roof. Whatever you're doing, on the job or off, you always give more than you take."

"The kitchen is a very funny place, but it's also pretty tough," Vinnie says. "If you show that somebody's joke got to you, or you make a mistake and then try to make excuses about it, you're gonna get your balls busted relentlessly. They just won't let up." That's good, he notes. "It keeps guys humble. It's like everybody's at the same level."

Besides a dormitory, Vinnie likens the firehouse to two other places. Both are traditionally male: a locker room and a military barracks. (In fact, he has heard that fighting a fire is "as close as you can get to warfare without going to war.") Athletics and the military are two institutions where, for decades, American society has permitted—in many cases, encouraged—homophobia to flourish. In these venues, homosexuality has been deemed incompatible with team building, anathema to good morale, destructive to group cohesiveness.

There is, however, one major difference between modern fire departments and their athletic and military counterparts: The fire force is still overwhelmingly white—and male.

Most firefighters, whether in large cities or small towns, come from blue-collar families. Many had fathers, uncles, and grandfathers who were firemen. When you are surrounded by people who look like you, Vinnie says, it is easy to think that everyone also acts and thinks like you.

"A guy who doesn't like black people knows not to say that in front of someone black, because it's socially unacceptable," Vinnie says. "But if he doesn't know anybody gay and assumes no one around him is, then he can say anything. And if no one says anything back when he does, it just sort of continues the idea that gay people can't be firemen."

Certainly, no one in command has ever told Vinnie's colleagues to knock off the antigay remarks. "If the bosses hear guys say shit about women or black firemen, they tell us to knock it off. But because everyone perceives there's no gay guys around, I've never heard anyone really stop saying it."

So antigay comments get thrown around the firehouse like hoses at a five-alarm blaze. Whether it is a reaction to a TV talk show ("Two mommies? That's fuckin' bullshit!") or a playful jest ("Look at that shit-eatin' grin. What guy sucked your dick last night?"), Vinnie is seldom out of earshot from an antigay remark.

Keeping quiet is difficult, he acknowledges. He would love to tell his fellow firefighters—the men for whom he would lay down his life, just as they would for him—that it is indeed possible to be masculine, a fireman, and gay. *Just look at me!* he sometimes wants to scream. Most of his colleagues are not stupid; while some are close-minded or ignorant, they are the minority. Part of Vinnie says, *I've proven myself; they like me, they know I'm a good fireman, so they'll be OK when I tell them.* But the other part of his brain counters, *Who are you kidding?* Then he thinks, *Once you're out, you're out forever. There's no turning back.* And that is the internal argument that continues to win the day.

Working under such stressful conditions has taken its toll on Vinnie. Whenever he thinks about coming out, he looks back at where he is and how he got there. In his mid 20s, he scored high on the fire department's difficult written examination and was one of only 450 candidates out of 27,000 to earn a perfect 100 on the physical test. He endured a long wait before his acceptance into a training class, then eagerly learned all he could about fire-fighting techniques and tactics. He came to work early and left late; he respected senior firefighters and worked holidays for them; he completed every mission, no matter how frightening, because it was the right thing to do and because every firefighter's life depends on every other firefighter.

Part of the stress Vinnie feels is because he was married when he joined the fire department. He had met a woman, and he loved her so much, he thought he could live the straight life he believed everyone in the world was living. But a couple of years later Vinnie's younger brother died suddenly, and he realized that life holds no guarantees. He had to be who he was. A year and a half later, after five years of marriage, he divorced his wife. Fearful the news would get back to the fire department, he never told her the true reason why.

Although his marriage was over and he wanted to acknowledge his sexuality, Vinnie never intended to come out publicly. "I wanted to live a lie, just not a married lie," he says. After the divorce Vinnie sank into a deep depression. He realized he finally had to deal with being gay, and he knew he needed another relationship—this time with a man.

Seeking solace, Vinnie turned to the Roman Catholic Church he had shunned while coming to terms with his own sexuality. A priest helped him confront his overwhelming guilt, and Vinnie regained his faith in God. "I realized He loves me, because He made me who I am," Vinnie says. The priest introduced him to other supportive priests and nuns. "People take shots at the church," Vinnie says. "All I can say is, I wouldn't be where I am today without it."

In his ongoing attempt to understand his homosexuality, Vinnie devoured books. One led him to Parents, Families, and Friends of Lesbians and Gays, or PFLAG. The organization put him in touch with a man who was once in a similar situation. He told Vinnie that coming out was a process, not an event. The man predicted that one day Vinnie too would rejoice in that process. "I thought he was nuts," Vinnie states.

Through his new friend he met two other gay men. For the first time he had a support system. He joined gay snowboarding, camping, and hiking clubs—groups he had no clue even existed. "I had never fit into the gay community," he says. "I'm very masculine, and I didn't find people like me in the bars. Being divorced didn't help either. A lot of gay people don't like that."

As his spirits rose and straight people around him noticed his change in demeanor, Vinnie realized he had to tell them why. The first person he came out to was his best friend. That man is now his ex–best friend. "He just couldn't deal with it or with me," Vinnie says sadly. He feels fortunate the man has not told anyone else.

Vinnie came out to his mother, stepmother, and stepsister. All were shocked but gave him support. It took a year before Vinnie told his father, a tough man who sometimes uttered homophobic epithets. He took the news better than Vinnie expected. To his surprise, Vinnie has not been disowned. (His brother, whom Vinnie told later, was supportive from the start.)

In fact, the relatively positive reactions of his relatives encouraged Vinnie to come out a bit more. Recognizing the mental gymnastics he had to perform every day just to remain in his self-imposed closet, Vinnie finally confided in a close, levelheaded friend at work. The man's initial response was surprising: He was convinced Vinnie was just rationalizing his divorce. When Vinnie convinced his colleague he truly was gay, the man accepted the information—and Vinnie.

Still, it took a year to come out to another firefighter. This time the reaction was different. The friend said, "I thought you were going to tell me something bad!" Emboldened, six months later Vinnie told a third coworker, "Patrick," and his wife. They said that if they had to list 100 people they thought were gay, Vinnie's name would not appear.

"Vinnie was already an established fireman," Patrick says. "He had taken me under his wing, like he did with so many other guys. We all wanted to be like Vinnie. I never had any idea he was gay. It was the biggest shock of my life for my wife and me. I mean, he was masculine, he was married…"

Vinnie's disclosure had a profound effect on Patrick. Subsequent conversations enabled him to understand that Vinnie did not choose to be gay; he was born that way. "I've got kids," Patrick says. "They're young, but years from now if they realize they're gay, I'll want them to be happy. I don't think it would bother me as much as it would have before I knew about Vinnie. And I know my wife and me are going to be very open with our kids."

But these affirming responses have not led to wholesale disclosures. The fact that three close colleagues know Vinnie's secret—and still like and respect him—is empowering, yet Vinnie is not ready to press his luck. The rest of the firefighters, he has decided, do not need to know.

The three firemen to whom he is out agree. "If Vinnie came out, it would be horrible," says Patrick. "His friends would always be his friends, but other people could be very, very cruel. The fact that he's a great fireman would help, but just one guy could make it awful for him. The fire department has been like his surrogate family, and if he came out, he could lose all that."

Since Vinnie came out to him, Patrick says, he has a new awareness of the firehouse culture. "In the kitchen, before, if the shoe didn't fit, I didn't notice. Now I hear everything that gets said, and a lot of times I feel horrible. Even if Vinnie isn't there, I feel bad when guys say stuff about gay people. If guys only knew there were gay people around them, they'd be shocked."

While his newfound knowledge gives him even greater appreciation of Vinnie—because he has to put up with so much more than other firefighters—Patrick is not yet ready to take a public stand against homophobia. "I'll say, 'Hey, whatever makes you happy,' but it ends there," he says, describing his reaction to antigay comments. "I don't want to push it because people might ask why I'm sticking up for gays. I'd like to speak out, but I guess I'm not strong enough."

In addition, in the fire department—at least at the station level, where it matters most—everyone knows that equal employment laws are ignored. The fire department remains one of the most conservative institutions in America.

"This place is very slow to change," Vinnie says. "Whether it's hiring or promoting or any other kind of policy, the idea is, If it works, don't change it." He acknowledges that because the firefighters hired today are, by and large, college educated, most have had more exposure to gay people and issues than senior members. "They're more open-minded at first, yeah," Vinnie says of his younger colleagues. However, that does not translate into institutional progress. "Once they get in the firehouse they hear all the bullshit, so they change. They're not as open as when they came in. Without even realizing it, they change."

He contrasts the fire department with the police force, which in recent years has made notable strides toward becoming more diverse. Most police departments now go out of their way to recruit women, blacks, Hispanics, and gays and lesbians. "That has a positive effect," he explains. "Because there are more minorities there, cops are used to working with people who are not the same. And I think there are just more people out there who want to be cops. The fire department has tried hard to recruit women and minorities, but it doesn't seem like anyone except white males wants this job."

Patrick, Vinnie's friend, agrees that police and firefighters are different. "Cops have to interact with the public; they see a lot of diversity. Whereas we go into a building, put out the fire, and don't really see the lives of the people who live there."

Patrick adds that firefighters feel they must maintain a macho image because of the nature of their work. "If you're running into a burning building, you can't back down. So if you show any sign of weakness, other guys in the department jump on it because they want to feel they can depend on you to save their life. And being gay in the fire department is a sign of weakness. If Vinnie came out, I think lots of guys—even the ones who know him and know he's a great fireman—might feel betrayed."

Gay police officers have created their own support organizations, and members march in gay pride parades. Firefighters seem to be afraid of forming a similar group and, as a result, have no public visibility. For years Vinnie believed he was the only gay fireman in the world. Gradually he has learned otherwise. He has met exactly two others; both were spectators at gay pride events in another city. (Vinnie will not attend a gay event in the city where he works and lives.) "We're sure there are others like us, but we're all so afraid of getting outed that we don't even want to get together," he says. "We all know we're in a precarious, uncomfortable situation."

Vinnie's discomfort extends to his social life. He is reluctant to tell gay people he meets how he makes his living, fearing the news might make it back to the firehouse. For the most part he lies, or says vaguely, "I work for the city." He recognizes, however, that dishonesty is not conducive to developing a strong relationship—something he aches for. As time goes on, he has taken more risks with new friends.

For a long time, the terror of running into someone he knew kept

Vinnie away from gay bars. Today, however, he realizes that anyone he sees would be there for the same reason he is. He also understands that he has the same right as every other human being to live a true life. It is a mark of how far he has come that he is now able to say, "I never want to be outed. But if I am, I hope my reputation and God will carry me through."

Vinnie knows that being a firefighter carries responsibilities—and creates stereotypes—unlike any other profession. No two tours are ever the same. One morning he might help save an entire family; that night he might lose his best friend. Firefighting is a team effort, enabling him to work intimately with "the finest people in the world—guys who would give me the shirt off their back, no questions asked." He knows fighting fires will never make him rich, but he cherishes the chance to spend his working life helping people.

Yet how can he explain all that to a man he just met in a gay bar? More times than he wishes to count, the reaction to meeting a fireman is "Do you guys really shower together?" or "Can I play with your hose?"

When he hears those comments, Vinnie says, "I'm outta there like a shot. That's someone I have no desire to talk to. That's what I mean when I say sometimes I don't fit in with the gay community. It's like even gay people don't understand that gay people can be firemen."

Someday, he believes, he will meet someone who loves him for who—not what—he is. "Being a fireman won't make a bit of difference" to that man, Vinnie hopes. "I'm a good person, and I'm fairly good-looking. I know God will make it happen."

Until that time, he battles more than the usual stress firemen face. Only on vacation, away from the firehouse, can Vinnie relax. "Reentry" is always hard. Recently, Vinnie says, it has become both easier and more difficult. The ease comes as he understands he deserves to live his life as a gay man. The difficulty arises, paradoxically, from his new openness. The more chances he takes, the riskier life gets. The conflict is enormous and ongoing.

As Vinnie knows, coming out is permanent. Still, he is doing so—slowly but steadily. Though he once called rejoicing in homosexuality "nuts," today he acknowledges, "I wouldn't *choose* to be gay, because of all the heartache we have to go through. But for the first time in my life, I'm me. And that's a good feeling to have."

Yet coming out completely and fully in the firehouse remains a fantasy. "I do think about it occasionally," Vinnie admits. "And I realize that when I finally meet someone to share my life with, when I've got everything going for me, I may not care as much about what I might have to go through at work."

Until then, though, he copes with the reality of the present. "Not a tour goes by that I don't hear at least one homophobic remark. Not one tour. So every day I go to work with that fantasy, and then I hear something and I realize it probably is just a fantasy."

Several years ago, after a heroic rescue, Vinnie was interviewed on the local news. His fellow firefighters, proud and emotionally pumped up, smiled for the cameras. Vinnie spent the next week nauseous, terrified he would be outed. Recently, however, he took part in another rescue. Again the television cameras descended on the firehouse. This time, knowing his secret is shared by a few colleagues, Vinnie was calmer. He basked in the same adulation his fellow firefighters enjoyed.

"I still hope no one outs me," he says. "But somebody might. If it happens, it happens. There's nothing I can do about it. No matter what happens, I know my life will go on. And I know, no matter what, I'll be OK."

Randy Culp: Oil Rig Mechanic

It was a casual comment, tossed off without thought in the middle of a busy workday on an oil rig anchored deep in the Gulf of Mexico: "Yeah, one time I let a guy suck my dick," one rig worker said to another. "Best blow job I ever had." It was part of normal, everyday conversation on the rig; seconds later, the speaker probably forgot he even said it.

Yet for Randy Culp—the man who heard it—the offhand remark was life-changing.

"That was an empowering comment for me," says the slow-talking mechanic in a Texas twang. "This ordinary guy on an oil rig admitted he'd had sex with a man. It was just an amazing comment to me."

As much as he wanted to, Randy could do nothing at that

moment. In those days, crews remained on their rig a week at a time. They worked 12-hour shifts, then had 12 hours off in quarters they shared with other men. Oil rigs are loud, active, sometimes dangerous places. The work is hard. Most men on an oil rig do not have much opportunity for—or interest in—male-to-male sex.

So Randy waited until he got back onshore. He had read rest-room walls; he knew where to go. Within a few months he had his first adult sexual encounter with another man. It took place in a public rest room and was very unsatisfying.

"He was about 60 and not someone I was physically attracted to," Randy recalls. "It was like smoking a cigarette: You know the first time isn't great, but you think maybe the next time will be."

It was. Randy soon began meeting young, attractive men. He liked them, and they liked the oil rig mechanic.

It was not long before he came out to his wife. She took it well. The couple had been together 11 years. She was a Baptist minister's daughter and thought homosexuality was a problem that could be fixed.

Randy knew better. He had gotten married at 19, when he had no clue who he was or what he wanted from life. His wife was the one who proposed; he'd agreed because in his small Texas town marriage seemed like the thing to do. The first seven years he was "quasi-happy." Later he resorted to fantasy to keep their sex life going. "Thank God," he says, "for Robert Redford in *The Way We Were*."

After his initial anonymous encounters, Randy had a fling that was more than just casual sex. His marriage disintegrated. His wife found another man, and the Culps divorced.

At the time they lived in a very small, rural Louisiana town. His ex-wife gossiped about Randy's boyfriend (without mentioning her own). The town was scandalized. She took their children—a son, then 9, and daughter, then 6—to Waco, Tex. Randy followed, hoping to remain part of their lives.

Though Waco is very conservative—Baylor, a strict Baptist university, dominates the area—there were pockets of liberalism. Randy, who does not like the bar scene, found a gay community through the

Unitarian Universalist Church. "I don't know whether my parents had more trouble with me being gay or a Unitarian Universalist," says this son and grandson of Baptist preachers. At the same time as he planned activities like a gay prom for teenagers, he battled for custody of his son. When the boy was a high school senior, Randy finally won.

Every couple of weeks Randy leaves Texas for the Gulf of Mexico. He works on a jack-up drilling rig—essentially, a barge that moves from spot to spot, jacks up, draws 5 million tons of seawater into its three legs, drills down for oil, then releases the water and moves somewhere else to do it all over again. For nearly a decade Randy has stayed with the same rig, owned by Ensco and contracted out to ExxonMobil.

He shares the rig with 50 men (and, very occasionally, one or two women). Many workers come and go, but Randy is permanent. He is the rig's mechanic, one of the best around. He monitors all equipment, particularly the three generators that provide the electricity needed to run the drilling equipment and maintain the three-story living quarters.

The rig is 270 feet long by 170 feet wide—about the size of a football field. Randy and his crewmates sleep on the second floor. Randy shares quarters with an electrician and welder. One man always works nights. Supervisory personnel live one floor above; the galley is below, along with a TV room, pool room, and weight room. It is, Randy says, "midway between grueling and comfortable."

The atmosphere is good—on Randy's rig, anyway. The crew is experienced and always scores high in both productivity and safety. There is a cohesive, cooperative atmosphere. He feels like a professional.

Of course, every rig is not like Randy's. His son, who also works offshore, was once threatened with death. The reason: His father is gay. "I'm very fortunate," Randy acknowledges. "Not everyone has the same working conditions I do. People get along very well here. Whenever there are so many people in such close quarters for such a long time, there will be conflicts. Everyone learns what everyone else's buttons are. It takes maturity not to push them out of spite. But we've got a mature crew here, and I appreciate that."

One button that others *could* push is the gay one. Randy calls himself "extremely out." Everyone on his rig knows he is gay. Getting to that point, though, has been a long process. For a while he was out only to an immediate supervisor and a few close friends. But then, in Waco, he met a man. They talked of marriage. On the rig there is a bulletin board where workers post personal news, usually about family events. Randy told a coworker he was thinking of adding his "marriage" news to everyone else's. The man told his prayer group. Someone from the group called the company's home office, asking that Randy be removed from the rig. The office called the rig to verify. A supervisor said that Randy had served on the rig a long time, had always been an excellent worker, and that removing him would not be a good idea. The home office agreed.

Now, whenever the company conducts diversity training, Randy's name comes up. As far as he knows, he is the only openly gay man working on an offshore oil rig—not just for Ensco but in the entire industry.

His son's experience is more typical, Randy says. "People on oil rigs are terrified of homosexuality. Most gay men don't want to work here. Gay guys who grow up in the backwoods of Alabama, Louisiana, Mississippi tend to take refuge in the big cities. We get the straight guys from rural America, guys with very poor educations in areas where there isn't a lot of industry or job opportunities. All of a sudden they find out they can work offshore and make a reasonably good livelihood. Where have they had a chance to meet or associate with gay people?"

One of Randy's roommates was a welder—and Ku Klux Klan member—from Alabama. "It was quite an experience for him to room with a gay person," says Randy. "He was there during my public coming-out period. We were friends before, and that strained our friendship to the breaking point. He's no longer with the company, but I find it gratifying that, for the rest of his life, this guy in the KKK will know that he was friends with a gay person. He won't be able to harm a gay person—and he's capable of it—without at least thinking about me."

The welder aside, most of Randy's close friends and coworkers reacted with a giant "So what?" They had known him awhile; he was an excellent mechanic; he had never come on to any of them. One supervisor said, "I don't approve of what you do at home, but I also don't care what you do there. Just do your job here." Randy thinks that is the way most people feel: As long as he keeps the machinery running, prevents problems from occurring, and makes everyone else on the rig look good, they're happy.

The sailing has not been entirely smooth, of course. "Fag" was scribbled on more than one wall, and Randy found homophobic Focus on the Family literature tacked to the bulletin board. Each time he took photographs and complained to supervisors, citing his company's sexual harassment policy. The graffiti and brochure-baiting ended and has not returned.

Now, Randy says, "the critical mass of people are accepting. Really, it's almost to the point of being affirming." His homosexuality is considered fair game for the routine ribbing that goes on whenever 50 men spend two weeks packed tightly in an environment Randy describes as "filled with free-floating testosterone."

"Come on, what really goes on with gay guys?" someone might taunt. "You can tell us."

"Join me," Randy retorts. "You might like it."

If he hears talk about "those cocksuckers," Randy quickly replies, "Hey, leave us cocksuckers out of this."

When the talk turns to sex, he is no longer afraid to say, "You should have seen it—I went out with the hottest marine!" Someone invariably responds, "Great, Randy, but we don't want to know." "Hey," he says, "every day I have to listen to your stories. You better listen to mine!"

And when he is in the workout room, lifting more weight than another man, he says with a smile, "Hey, fuckin' pussy, how does it feel gettin' beat out by a queer?"

Over the years Randy has made some seemingly odd acquaintances. For instance, a Mormon driller who supervises a crew of roughnecks has become one of Randy's strongest supporters. "He finds me interesting to talk to," Randy says. "He likes the books and foreign films I bring with me. He tells people I give him his dose of culture and class."

One thing that does not occur on his oil rig is sex—at least as far as Randy is aware. "You'd think I'd be the first to know. Then again, maybe guys avoid me because I'm so much in the spotlight." He has been approached several times—primarily by straight men, he says, although maybe a couple of them were bisexual—but because of his visibility he avoids any compromising activity. The men on a rig who look for sex tend to move on, he says. The ones who remain are better workers because they're not spending all their time trying to hook up.

Now at the end of what he calls "a long, stressful process," Randy looks back and recognizes the toll that coming out took on his personal productivity and, as a result, the entire rig's. When the Focus on the Family pamphlets were being distributed, Randy knew that many coworkers read and believed the inaccurate information. He spent a great deal of time trying to undo misperceptions. "That took a tremendous effort," he says. "When you're working that close to people 12 hours at a time, you have to have a good relationship. If there's a conflict looming over your head, it can't help but affect your concentration or timing or judgment. So if people have the right information and they're not homophobic, it doesn't interfere with your work." Randy is pleased that during team building exercises, ExxonMobil stresses that time spent developing good working relationships is not wasted time.

These days, when he is not on the rig, Randy lives in Austin. The men he meets are attracted to him because he is in good physical condition. But many are turned off when they learn he is a blue-collar worker. Recently he fell in love with a psychologist. A marriage counselor pronounced them evenly matched, having no power differential. Still, Randy says, "for a lot of gay people, a mechanic has less value than someone with a college or professional degree. And working my schedule—two weeks on, two weeks off—makes it hard to develop a relationship." (That last point also holds true for straight men on the rig, he notes.)

When Randy went offshore for the first time, in 1980, he told himself he would stay for a year. Later, he planned to remain until his children got out of college. Now, in his mid 40s, he makes good money and is building a nice retirement package. He likes his work situation—what he does and who he does it with—and sees no reason to switch careers. "When I was in the closet and then just coming out, I was desperate to change," he says. "Now my work life and home life are integrated. I'm not looking to change a thing."

His gay and family lives are finally integrated too. Both of his children came to the recent gay prom he helped organize. While attending a conservative high school, his son Kirby joined Junior ROTC—and was out about having a gay dad. Randy helped the JROTC group organize Texas Trash-out Day. Kirby's friends always felt welcome at Randy's house. Several have since joined the Marines. One described his military training: "They tried to tell me all this shit about gay guys, but I just said, 'Not the gay people I know.' "

That is something Randy Culp will always cherish. Which makes it almost as memorable as the comment he heard 15 years ago—the life-changing one his coworker made about the best blow job he ever got.

"DOUG": PRISON GUARD

It takes a certain kind of man to be a prison guard. You've got to like power, feel comfortable carrying a weapon, and not be afraid to use it on another human being. You thrive on tension and keep cool in pressure situations. You know danger lurks around every dingy corner, but you love the opportunity to make independent decisions—and see immediate, tangible results. You enjoy acting in control, even if you're not always sure you are. You derive pleasure from playing mind games with inmates and don't mind when they try to do the same with you. You find it intriguing trying to figure out their unique society. You appreciate the little perks (free coffee at the local diner) and love the money (with ample overtime, it adds up quickly). Most of all, you draw energy from the intense bonds you form with your colleagues.

Prison guards, perhaps more than any other workers, trust each other with their lives. "I got your back" is a literal, not figurative, expression. When you can be attacked any time, without warning—and are constantly outnumbered by angry, violent, trapped men—you must have complete and utter faith in your partner. You hope, of course, that your partner feels the same about you. The best—in fact, the only—way to ensure that trust is by acting just as confident, just as strong, just as macho as everyone else.

Which means you absolutely, positively, cannot—under any circumstances—be gay.

"Doug" learned that lesson well. A 5-foot-10, 265-pound sheriff's deputy in charge of 120 inmates at a county correctional facility in Massachusetts, he saw what happened when a sergeant was outed as a lesbian. Because she had rank, no one said anything to her face. But from that moment on, no one lifted a finger to help her either. "Fuck her. Let her sit," guards said as she waited perilously at gates to exit a cellblock. She lost her friends. Eventually she quit. She never faced a riot situation, but Doug knew that if she did, her coworkers would have been excruciatingly slow to cover her back.

He knows too that he might have been just as slow to come to her aid. Even though Doug is gay and knew the sergeant to be a good officer, he treated her as poorly as those around him did, chuckling at every cruel joke, offering no support. "No way could I come to her defense," he says. "Someone would ask, 'Why are you on *her* side?' If you side with someone on the outs, you push yourself to the outs. Everything in a prison environment is 'us' against 'them.' It's not only the inmates that have a hierarchy. The guards do too. And ours is just as tough as theirs."

Hierarchical societies hold a certain comfort for Doug. A Boston-area native who grew up in a well-off family and attended an all-boys Catholic school, he joined the Army ROTC immediately after enrolling at a small Massachusetts college in fall 1993. The intensity of the program appealed to him; so did the strictness of the Uniform Code of Military Justice. He thrilled to the physical and psychological challenges. "They gave us impossible tasks to accomplish in far too little time," he recalls, "but we did it. We'd pop off M-60 rounds on the shooting range and jump out of airplanes. Then I'd go back to school and say, 'What did *you* do this weekend?' " He formed close bonds with his fellow cadets and looked up to the officers whose ranks he hoped to join one day. "I loved the people," he says. "Of course, if they'd known about me, they might not have loved me."

Homosexuality was nothing new to Doug. He realized he was gay when he was 7 or 8 yet never felt conflicted. Still, he knew that being gay was unacceptable in his popular jock crowd, so he kept it a secret.

Doug remained closeted in ROTC, in college classes, and on the varsity football team, which he joined in his freshman year as a walk-on (that is, he wasn't recruited to the team), immediately earning a starting defensive tackle spot. With a 56-inch chest, bench-pressing 500 pounds, no one ever suspected he was gay—and Doug aimed to keep it that way. To this day he is officially out only to his mother, though he realizes his two brothers—one a policeman, the other the vice president of an international company—have discussed it behind his back.

Double-majoring in political science and English, Doug knew he would wind up in either business or law enforcement. One brother had worked in the county sheriff's department, so as a 19-year-old sophomore Doug had an important "in." "I needed beer money, and that paid a king's ransom for a college kid," he says. Working three nights a week during school, five in the summer (on top of a day job), Doug earned $30,000 his first year.

That bought plenty of beer, but it was not easy money. Doug was responsible for the direct supervision of inmates—sometimes at a hospital, more often in a two-tiered cellblock. He and a partner patrolled a 40-yard-long, 20-yard-wide corridor. Inmates either roamed or hung out in a dayroom furnished only with couches, card tables, and one television set.

It was a power trip. "Hey, I'm 19 and a prison guard, a sworn officer with arrest powers," he said about that time. "I had the same authority as a police officer anywhere in the county, and in my cellblock I had supreme authority over when guys could eat, sleep, talk, or shit. That's a head trip for anyone."

The work environment was good. Corrections officers are a notoriously cliquish group, but because Doug walked in on his brother's coattails, he was quickly accepted. And the commander gave his guards the run of the place. "He always said, 'If you think it's the right call, you make it,' " Doug says. "Your cellblock was yours to run. No one stepped on your dick." There was constant joking; the atmosphere was as fun as any jail could be.

Still, it *was* a prison. Inside "the perimeter," guards carried radios and handcuffs but no guns, mace, or batons—weapons that could, in the wrong circumstances, be used against them. That is why the trust of coworkers is such a crucial component of the job.

"As soon as someone doesn't trust you, you run the risk of losing your life," Doug explains. "We had arson, assaults, race riots in there. When that happens you need immediate response. If you're on the outs, you won't get it." A guard may find himself or herself on the outs for any number of reasons. Ratting on a fellow officer is one. Another is not going along with the crowd. A third is being gay.

"These aren't the brightest people in the world," Doug says of prison guards. "There's a lot of regular, blue-collar guys who barely got through high school. They're not particularly enlightened. If I came out, they couldn't have really thought through the situation— 'Hey, he's the same guy he was before.' They don't really think like that."

That is why, as often as he could, Doug made sure his colleagues saw him hitting on women in bars and then taking them home. He accompanied his coworkers to strip joints, always making the appropriate leering comments about tits. There was plenty of talk about sports too (a topic Doug did not have to fake). Playing straight was not difficult. After all, he'd been doing it his entire life.

The downside was that Doug did not spend a lot of time in the gay world. He avoided bars, terrified he would see someone he knew. (It did not dawn on him until later that they would be there for the same reason he was.) He dated a man for two years, but when discussing his relationship he always changed pronouns. None of the other guards ever met "Janet"; she always seemed to be away on business.

In some ways, prisoners were more tolerant of homosexuality than Doug's coworkers. Jammed into a building built for 500, the 1,000 or so inmates—primarily Hispanic, serving time for crimes ranging from driving while intoxicated to rape, murder, and child molestation—included two who were openly gay, Doug recalls. One was a transvestite who wanted to be called Tricia. "She had every stereotype: a lisp, swish, you name it," Doug says. "I was interested in how the inmates would react. There was a lot of joking, but it was good-natured—nothing like the other officers and the lesbian sergeant. These guys are street thugs, gangbangers, but it was no big deal. They didn't need to cause undue problems over things; they had bigger fish to fry. He was a total femme, unthreatening, so no one could get any juice from harassing him. You get that from the tougher guys. There's no points for taking out a total fish." The second openly gay inmate was certifiably crazy. He masturbated while yelling Doug's partner's name and spent most of his time segregated from other inmates.

In the prison hierarchy, sexual orientation matters little. Gay men are not considered particularly low; that status belongs to child molesters and rapists. "The thinking goes, 'What kind of pussy has to pick on a kid or a woman?'" explains Doug. Cop killers stand at the top of the heap, with other murderers close behind.

As might be expected in an all-male population, sexual activity does take place. Early one morning Doug glanced at a security camera monitor near his desk and saw two men going at it hot and heavy. "Sexual contact is clearly against the rules," he says. "I nudged my partner. He got pissed and hauled them off in leg irons. I just told them they were pretty stupid. It was consensual, but it was against regulations, so I couldn't let it slide."

Sometimes, making rounds late at night, Doug would hear suggestive noises. Unless he caught inmates having sex outright, he did nothing, though he had been trained to keep an eye out for young, thin inmates spending time with older, more established ones and had been instructed to follow them if they "disappeared" together. Sex in prisons, both consensual and otherwise, does occur, but far less than popular fantasy suggests, according to Doug.

Despite his enjoyment of his job—the power, independence, and pressure—the appeal faded as he grew older. "I had to do things in there that, if I did them on the outside, would have landed me in jail," he says without elaboration. "The environment was not good. I realized I was working with small-minded people who, if they found out about me, would not speak to me during my whole shift." In college and through travel, his mind was opened to new ideas; he looked at his coworkers and saw a narrow band of life experience. Every night after work they retreated to the same bar, downed the same drinks, told the same stories, and laughed at the same jokes.

Any new idea, event, or person was viewed as a threat. Part of that reaction came from the nature of prison work. A person who must act macho and tough every single minute on the job develops defense mechanisms that shut out anything different. Such a person builds barriers to prevent anyone who might not fit that protective self-image from intruding. Prison guards are not inherently bad people, Doug stresses. In fact, many are "genuinely good human beings who are, unfortunately, unequipped by their job and background to act any way other than badly. They're blue-collar guys who come from families and environments where prejudice rules, and they're in a line of work that says, 'No one puts anything over on me. I've got a gun, and I have to act manly.' "

Slowly Doug realized he was becoming one of "them." After five years, at the end of one particularly bad day punctuated by a particularly bad fight, he'd had enough. He bought a ticket to Florida, decompressed for six weeks, returned to Massachusetts, and took a job with a bank. His new peace of mind was more than worth his 50% pay cut, he says.

Looking back, he realizes his life is filled with parallels. Prison, the military, athletics—all are worlds in which he struggled every day to prove his manhood. In the middle of a cellblock riot he stood his ground until help arrived. In the Army he was graded on strength.

And in football, the only way he could get on the field was to be tougher than his teammates.

"My life does have a common thread of toughness and homogeneity," Doug admits. "I've been in countless jailhouse brawls and never lost one. I competed in bench press competitions, I wrestled and played lacrosse, and I won a hell of a lot. But in all those things, if people knew I was gay, my standing would have been diminished. The simple fact that I suck dick would have made me less of a man. I'd just be one sick pervert."

In such an overwhelmingly traditional, macho world, can a prison guard ever be openly gay? "Absolutely not," Doug says unhesitatingly. "I had a hell of a lot of laughs, I learned a lot, and I loved most of my time there. But that environment is one where you need absolute, unquestioned trust in the person next to you, and gay people are simply not going to be trusted. The prejudice against gay people is totally ingrained. And it's not going to go away, because the job of human zookeeper is not going to start attracting educated people. I don't foresee the day when someone is going to go to college to learn to be a prison guard."

Hypothetically, what if Doug came out—say, by using his real name in this book? "First, there would be utter disbelief," he predicts. "People outside of prison don't believe I'm gay to begin with—when I go in a bar, I practically have to kiss a guy to prove it—so they wouldn't believe that at all. Next, I'd be a huge topic of discussion. Then I'd be persona non grata. I'd switch from being someone they'd buy a beer for into someone they'd cross the street to avoid."

But wouldn't at least one person's attitude change? "I'd bet my next five paychecks against it," Doug counters adamantly. "Prison work is a zero-sum game. You're either with us or against us. If anyone stood up for me, he'd be standing up for all gay people, and no one would ever trust that man again. You have to understand: As a prison guard, you spend eight hours a day with the guys you work with. And to those guys, those eight hours are the most important thing in the world."

MARK WEBER, PAUL BLOOM, MAX SCHNEIDER: DOCTORS

Mark Weber

As a doctor specializing in pediatric and adolescent medicine, Mark Weber's job consists of far more than treating colds and administering physicals. One reason he chose his specialty is because it allows him to get to know his patients and their families well. He believes a doctor's job is not just to cure illness but to help prevent it—and, equally important, to educate young people so they can grow into physically and emotionally healthy adults.

For as long as he was interested in medicine, Mark wanted to deliver primary care. The preventive aspect of the pediatric and adolescent specialty was particularly appealing. "When people are young, you can influence their habits a lot more easily than when they're older. With adults, all you can do is change bad habits," he explains. He wants his patients to take responsibility for their own health. When they are 8 years old he provides information on cigarettes, alcohol, and drugs. As they grow older he includes sexuality in their talks.

When talking with early adolescents, Mark routinely describes the changes that will soon buffet their bodies. In scrupulously nonjudgmental tones he tells them that soon they may be attracted to boys, girls, both, or neither. A youngster occasionally giggles; a boy blurts out that of course he likes girls. "Well, I can't assume," Mark says simply. "Some boys don't."

One mother was taken aback by Mark's approach. Curtly she informed him that the longer her son went without hearing such a thing, the less likely he would be to choose that option. She asked the physician to promise not to talk about homosexuality again and to place a note in her son's chart signifying that.

Mark refused. He explained he was not promoting same-sex feelings; he was merely explaining them as part of any adolescent doctor's educational mission. It was no different from explaining acne, depression, or any other fact of human existence. He would not compromise her son's care by ignoring or glossing over facts all young people should hear.

Mark expected the woman to remove her family from the group practice he was affiliated with. However, she did not; her husband convinced her that Mark had placed no value judgments on homosexuality. The family stayed.

Coincidentally, that same day Mark described the same feelings the same way to another young adolescent. His mother's reaction was more gratifying: "Thank you. I'm glad you're talking about these issues. They are so important for my son to hear."

Though he knows, even more than most doctors, how important it is, Mark Weber does not always find it easy to address gay topics. A private man by nature, the 45-year-old is out to colleagues and other professionals but not to most patients. He does not consider it important for them or their parents to know he is gay, just as he does not think they need to learn about any personal aspect of any doctor's life.

His job, he says, is to serve their health needs, and that has nothing to do with his sexuality.

Yet he is hardly closeted. On his desk he displays a photograph of himself and his partner, Howard, who works in computers. "Oh, you have a brother," one patient remarked. "No, he's a friend," Mark replied. Later that day, reflecting on the incident, Mark realized that while he always expects his patients to be truthful, he himself had not been. He phoned the patient and asked if he really wanted to know who Howard was. The young man did, so Howard told him. It made absolutely no difference in their doctor-patient relationship.

Since his commitment ceremony Mark has worn a ring. Patients now assume he is married and ask if he has children. Mark says no but adds no other information. "What purpose would that serve?" he asks. "It would seem gratuitous to me. My job is to educate them in the context of *their* medical concerns. It's not about me."

Of course, education takes many forms. One day Mark entered the examining room to find a teenage boy who had not donned a paper gown. Mark informed the youngster that if he felt embarrassed, he did not have to.

"Well, it's not a problem unless the doctor's gay," the boy responded.

Surprised, Mark asked, "Isn't how someone *acts* more important than what they are?"

The boy mulled the question over for a few seconds. "I guess you're right," he replied.

Still, Mark admits at times he would like to take the educational process further. He would not mind saying, "Look at me. I'm a gay man in this profession. You didn't know, so why should you care?" However, he cannot do it without drawing attention to himself. That means shifting the focus away from his patients. And that is not the role Mark sees for himself as a doctor.

Mark, who lives with Howard in the suburbs 20 miles from his Boston practice, does not try to hide their relationship. Yet neither does he flaunt it. "I've often wondered what would happen if all my families knew," he muses. "I hope it wouldn't be a problem or make a difference. But I'm not sure. They do know I'm open-minded, and I've got gay-supportive materials in my office. But I don't know how many of them have connected that to my being gay, and I'm not sure that it matters."

While Mark does not believe he faces any substantive issues a straight doctor would not, he feels that being gay makes him especially sensitive to patients who see themselves as existing outside society's mainstream. He has helped youngsters who feel "out of it" understand that eventually they will find their niche. To his satisfaction, boys and girls he sees only once or twice a year take that message to heart.

Interestingly, Mark's own sexuality had a profound influence on him when he was young. For a time, it nearly kept him from reaching his full potential. He was born in New York City, then at age 5 moved with his parents to suburban White Plains. In retrospect, he realizes that on some level he always felt different from other children. Though a good runner, he was never particularly interested in sports. He also never went through a typical preadolescent "girl-hating" phase. In junior high he was shy, yet popular enough to be drafted to run for class president.

That was around the time one classmate pegged Mark as gay. He was not harassed outright, but whispers followed him around. One day Mark sent two Mets tickets to someone he desperately wanted to befriend. The boy tore them into tiny pieces, then returned them with a scathing note: "It's bad enough to be a fairy, but to be an annoying one is worse." Thirty years later Mark still has the torn-up tickets and note. They serve as searing reminders of some youngsters' astonishing cruelty—and others' terrible vulnerability.

Mark calls his years at White Plains High School "not particularly enjoyable." His parents realized he was lonely but had no idea why. He adamantly refused their request to see a therapist. His grades never suffered; he did not drink or do drugs; he made friends through the American Field Service and was well respected. Still, he considered himself an outsider. He did not attend his senior prom.

He chose Hobart College in upstate New York, partly because he knew no one there; it was a place to make a fresh start. His first roommate was dissimilar—a soccer player and wrestler—but they got along well. Mark majored in chemistry and graduated with a 3.7 grade point average. Hobart was good for him—to a point. As a freshman he had promised himself he would be more sociable and, thinking his same-sex attractions were a phase, he looked forward to meeting the perfect girl. Of course, no human being is perfect. Whenever Mark met a woman, he managed to find a reason not to continue dating her.

Mount Sinai School of Medicine in Manhattan represented an enormous transition. Thrown in with a class full of high achievers, Mark nonetheless managed to find a group of friends. Early in their first year another student came out to him. Even though by that time Mark had had several sexual encounters with men, he refused to admit to himself or his friend that he was gay. He continued to wait for the perfect woman. (To this day, that man is the only other member of his 200-person class whom Mark knows definitely to be gay.)

After medical school, Mark was assigned to a residency program at Children's Hospital of Buffalo. Transitions have always been difficult for him, and in midwinter—cold, lonely, stressed, depressed, burnt out from working the respiratory floor with infants—he asked his supervisor for another rotation. Before reassignment he was required to see a therapist. Those meetings were significant because of what he thought but did not say. "I self-censored," he recalls. "I couldn't tell anyone I wanted a close relationship with another man." But Mark ended counseling knowing there was a major issue he had to face sooner or later.

He learned about a gay student group at nearby State University of New York and with great trepidation attended his first meeting. He circled the building 10 times before gathering the courage to walk in. But once inside, he met a man who invited Mark to his apartment, and there he saw a woman he had treated on rotation. She was the first straight person to know Mark was gay. To his vast relief, she did not care.

Gradually he met other gays and lesbians at the hospital, and his long coming-out process accelerated. He found his first boyfriend, and his second. Not until after his second breakup, however, did Mark enter a gay bar. For a long time he felt bars were too public for him. But late one rainy Saturday night he took the risk. He stood awkwardly inside for a while. Eventually a man said hello. They talked, and Mark went home with him. That night was the first time Mark self-identified as gay, a major turning point in his life.

The more comfortable he became with himself, the more he ventured out. The bolder he became, the more people from the hospital he saw. He also learned to figure out which colleagues were gay but—like himself just a few months earlier—unable to summon the courage to come out.

In fall 1983, as he began his third year of residency, Mark attended a family function with his parents. On the way home he told them: "You know, there's always been a lot of tension between us. We never talk deeply about anything. Well, I want to clear the air. I'm gay."

Their first concern was for his career. They could not understand how a gay man could choose—let alone be accepted in—pediatric and adolescent medicine. They offered to support him in any different residency and fellowship program he wanted. Their suggestions for "safe" specialties were dermatology and geriatrics.

No, Mark told them. Working with children and teenagers is what he wanted to do. He was good at it, and he planned to continue doing so.

In truth, he shared some of his parents' worries. But he wanted to be in primary care preventive medicine and to help youngsters. No matter what obstacles he faced, he would do it.

During his adolescent-medicine fellowship at Boston's New England Medical Center, Mark discovered that being gay was not a big deal. Because most patients do not believe their doctors have lives outside the office, they cannot conceive of the fact that they have any kind of sexuality at all.

It helped that teenagers travel in social circles separate from doctors. Once, however, during "gay night" at a Boston roller rink, he ran into a boy he had treated at an adolescent clinic. Suddenly Mark had to decide whether to acknowledge his patient or hide. The decision was made for him when the boy approached Mark and asked why he was there. "A friend invited me," Mark said truthfully. "Me too," the youth replied. Mark felt thankful such encounters were rare.

Throughout his fellowship Mark's parents worried that someone would accuse him of improper behavior. At their urging he came out to his director, who offered to speak to Mark's parents himself. They traveled to Boston, where the director told them every doctor risks being accused of anything. Gays, he said, are no more imperiled than any other physician.

That eased Mark's parents' fears, but still they wanted him to confer with another professional: a man who claimed to have "cured" homosexuals. Reluctantly Mark agreed but on one important condition: If he went, his parents had to attend a PFLAG meeting. Mark and his parents quickly realized the doctor's "cure" was not what it seemed. It took another two years, though, before they held up their end of the bargain and actually made it to PFLAG. As soon as they joined, however, they became comfortable with both the organization and their son's homosexuality. More than a decade later they remain active, committed PFLAG parents.

After Mark's fellowship he joined the Northeastern University health center. Several doctors and nurses realized he kept moving to different apartments with the same man, and a lesbian nurse remarked that it was great having him on staff because most doctors were not gay-supportive.

Mark did not feel the need to come out to most student patients; however, he framed all his questions to them in gender-neutral, open-ended ways ("If you're having sex, does your partner...?"). If they responded in kind, he followed up more specifically. Occasionally he came out. One memorable gay patient was working on an engineering degree but planned to become a bartender. Mark thought that was an important time to be open, to show the student that being gay did not automatically limit his career options.

Six years later, drawn by the opportunity to treat adolescents, Mark joined a general medical practice. The teenage years, he says, are when vital physical and psychological development takes place. He was out to his fellow doctors and office staff from the start, without a problem. Yet, repeating his Northeastern University experience, he was not out to most patients—not even a boy with stress-related stomach pains who came out to him. "What purpose would it have served?" Mark asks. "He might have gotten the idea I was gay, because I was so comfortable talking about it, but our discussions weren't about me, they were about him. My life had nothing to do with his. In fact, considering the sexuality of his provider might have scared him."

Mark continued his out-to-colleagues, quiet-with-patients approach for several years, with a few exceptions. One occurred when a PFLAG family sought him out, hoping their gay son could have a positive role model. He happily agreed.

A typical day for Mark consists of seeing children and young adults. Some come with their parents, others without. He performs routine exams, treats minor illnesses, and deals with urgent matters including injuries, sexually transmitted diseases, and emotional problems. His patients' questions range from the safety of steroids to the wisdom of certain career choices. But Mark communicates in other ways too. His office is filled with PFLAG information, and he has hung a PFLAG poster in the bathroom. That way, people can surreptitiously copy the phone number.

Mark is unsure how his sexuality relates to his work as an adolescent doctor. He knows that, at some level, being gay is an integral part of who he is, yet he does not consider himself much different from straight physicians. He does admit that his long process of accepting his sexual orientation has made him more sensitive than most doctors to the emotional needs of his patients and their families. Once reserved and shy, he now feels comfortable discussing all areas of life, from bodily functions to emotional difficulties. That, he feels, creates an environment that allows young patients to talk with him about any issue that impacts health: alcoholism, sexual abuse, parental pressure—even, occasionally, homosexuality.

Though only a few patients have come out, Mark does not think that reflects on him. Some adolescents, he says, have not yet realized they are gay; others who do know may self-select a specialized health care facility for gays, lesbians, bisexuals, and the transgendered.

Besides, he says, being a gay adolescent physician is not about numbers. It is not about treating gay patients or even being out himself. It *is* about providing important health and emotional care to a vulnerable, dynamic, and educable segment of the population—straight and gay—that desperately needs it. And that is something he could not have done had he heeded the pleas of his once fearful parents and become Mark Weber, dermatologist.

Paul Bloom

Paul Bloom is a 56-year-old pediatrician who loves practicing community medicine. He makes no effort to hide his sexuality. He believes being out is important, though he feels no need to identify himself as a "gay physician" every time he asks a patient to say "A-a-ah."

Like Mark, Paul was a high achiever. Unlike Mark, however, Paul took a long time before acknowledging his attraction to men. The valedictorian of his high school on New York's Long Island, he attended Amherst College when it was all-male. Contemporary books and articles described homosexuality as a phase of immaturity most people outgrow. He has since learned that many of his fraternity brothers are gay. Back then, of course, no one discussed it.

In 1963 friends introduced Paul to a student at all-female Smith College, and in his second year at the Bronx's Albert Einstein College of Medicine they were married. Paul held romantic notions about both matrimony and medicine. As an undergraduate English major he had read a story about a doctor saving a pneumonia patient's life and thought that was what the profession would be like. It took him awhile to realize that medicine is no different than any other business.

But first came the Lincoln Collective, a political group of hippies and revolutionaries at Lincoln Hospital in the poverty-stricken South Bronx. Organized in 1970, the collective practiced "social medicine." They wanted to meld good health care with political principles in a community direly in need of both. Paul learned Spanish, and his wife grew active in the collective's feminist wing.

"We were 'small c' communists," Paul explains. "It was an exciting time. We had sit-ins in hospital offices, trying to get better care, and we donated money to the Young Lords [an organization dedicated to gaining human rights for U.S. Latinos and to liberating Puerto Rico] to help them achieve their political goals. We did good things. We talked about everything—except homosexuality. That was the only taboo. Now I know that a lot of us were gay. We laugh about it today, but for me that was a bittersweet time."

Paul spent nearly six years in the South Bronx. When the Lincoln Collective broke up, he stayed on as an attending physician. His colleagues moved to places like Appalachia; finally he relocated to Rockland, New York State's smallest county, which sits bucolically and affluently on the Hudson River, north of New York City. Paul was drawn there by an advertisement for a bilingual physician. He chose to work in Haverstraw, a lively, proud city filled with immigrants from Puerto Rico, the Dominican Republic, and Ecuador.

In 1977 his health care center went broke, so Paul entered private practice. He hated the capitalist model of medicine—and still does—so he made do with a small office staff of three doctors and a nurse practitioner.

In Rockland County he came to terms with his sexuality. Despite more than two decades of marriage, his attraction to men had not waned. On Valentine's Day 1987, National Public Radio aired an interview with John McNeill, a gay priest recently removed by the Vatican. When the Rev. McNeill called himself a "celibate homosexual," Paul nearly drove off Route 59. At age 42 he suddenly understood that homosexuality was not about who you have sex with but rather who you are.

He told his wife the news. They decided to deal with it the best way they knew: politically. He became an activist with the nearest gay community center, the Loft, across the river in Westchester County. He helped organize fund-raisers and start a youth group. As with much of his political activity, he calls it "great fun."

Paul and his wife never divorced—a decision that, he says, upsets many gay friends. (His two grown children, who were told as teenagers, have always been supportive.) But he did move to Nyack, which he describes as an "offbeat village." It is artsy, yet home to a substantial number of evangelical Christians.

In 1994 a reporter for the local paper asked Paul for his thoughts on the 25th anniversary of the Stonewall riots. He expected his words to appear in a small article on a back page. Instead the story ran on page 1—accompanied by his photo.

"Oh, shit!" he thought. "Now my life is really going to change." He had already come out to his two business partners, both Indians. The men—one a Muslim, the other Hindu—told him he was a good doctor. They did not think his revelation would hurt their practice. Paul asked if they wanted someone else present when he examined young patients. Of course not, they scoffed. The issue has not arisen since.

A few evangelical families went elsewhere, and one or two people asked if he had AIDS. Nearly everyone else, however, has been accepting. The reaction of a poor white family was typical. The father—an enormous, tattooed laborer—greeted him the first time after the newspaper story with the words, "Doc, I'm really pissed off."

Paul waited nervously for whatever came next.

With mock seriousness the man continued: "How come you never made a pass at me?" It was his way of acknowledging Paul as a caring physician; the doctor's sexuality was irrelevant.

Like Mark Weber's, Paul's office is adorned with posters proclaiming the wonders of diversity. He has become a resource for parents and patients with questions about homosexuality, and has drawn several same-sex couples with children to his practice. In his side work, teaching residents at Nyack Hospital, he gives physicians-in-training information about gay youth they have never before heard. For that they are grateful.

As a pediatrician in a small town who treats patients from birth to age 21, Paul knows people well. When boys and girls reach 13 he tells them directly to ask anything they want; his office, he says, is private and confidential. Very few teenagers jump at his offer—not right then, anyway. Eventually, though, some do. A young Hispanic boy, for example, admitted that the reason he'd been beaten up was because he is gay. Paul began treating the boy's psyche as well as his injuries. Another youngster, very religious, tentatively admitted to dreaming about boys. Gently and nonjudgmentally, but at great length, Paul told him how normal such feelings are.

Still, in neither of those situations did Paul out himself. He thinks patients know he is gay—after all, he wears an earring *and* a rainbow pin, and he even talks about his work with the Loft's Center Lane youth group—but he feels it is inappropriate to mention his own sexuality when dealing with others'.

As a gay pediatrician, Paul knows he does not have much company. Of the nearly 2,000 members of the Gay and Lesbian Medical Association (a group that only recently, and after much debate, changed its name from the more innocuous-sounding American Association of Physicians for Human Rights), only about 75 are listed under "Pediatrics." "People worry about being accused of things," Paul says. "That's ridiculous. If I was straight, would anyone think I was staring at teenage girls? Any doctor knows a medical exam is not a sexual situation. I can't be paranoid about things like that."

In the next breath, however, Paul admits he might not encourage a young doctor just finishing residency to come out. He believes it is valuable to be accepted first as a good physician. He notes that of 300 staff doctors at Nyack Hospital, he is the only one who is openly gay. He says, "That's ridiculous. I can't speak for other people, but I think in my generation, gay doctors have a lot of internalized homophobia. I would advise [established doctors] to just be out and answerable to their own behavior. If you are good at what you do, people will trust you."

Max Schneider

In the late '50s, when Paul Bloom was just a teenager and Mark Weber was still in elementary school, Max Schneider was one of the best known, most successful, and most beloved physicians in Buffalo, N.Y. His internal medicine practice was booming. His work on a new form of artificial respiration, called mouth-to-mouth resuscitation, had earned nationwide praise. His latest interest, alcoholism-related diseases and treatment, was opening even more professional doors. His activities as a second responder for the fire and police departments were both exciting and beneficial. A former Eagle Scout who continued to work with the Boy Scouts of America, he received the Silver Beaver Award, the highest honor a local council can bestow. And he was gay.

Though Max had never come out publicly, he did not have to. The people who knew he was gay supported him fully; no one else needed to know. His cottage, just across the Niagara River in Canada, was a popular meeting place for countless gay men (even a few lesbians) in the area.

But one night in 1959, on his way home from a medical call—while driving his car with a police radio and siren, searching for a sexual encounter—Max picked up a vice officer and was arrested. What happened next seems, four decades later, humorous. From jail he called his parents—two of the few people who did not know he was gay—and broke the news. "Why didn't you tell us before?" they asked. "I didn't want you to know I was dating a non-Jew," he replied.

Other things happened too, however, and they were not so humorous. The head of the vice squad was a patient of Max's and succeeded in getting the charge dismissed because Max was researching a book. But one of the local papers printed a story about the dropped charges, and soon the head of the local Boy Scouts of America council called. He suggested Max resign his position on the board of directors, which he did.

Amazingly, the only two patients Max lost were the newspaper reporter who wrote the story and the reporter's wife. (Perhaps, Max chuckles, the reason was that he began charging them $100 for $5 visits.) Several patients even came out to him after learning he was gay.

The arrest and ensuing publicity did not drive Max out of

Buffalo. He continued to do what he had always done: "Be honest, practice good medicine, and be available." His patients still loved him, he continued his important research into addictions, and his cottage in Canada remained a popular weekend social refuge.

But Max was not getting any younger. At age 41 his native city's notorious weather was wearing him down. On November 23, 1963, the night after President John F. Kennedy's assassination, Max made a house call in a blinding snowstorm. On the way there he came to a momentous decision: He would put his practice and cottage up for sale and move to California.

As quickly as he decided, however, he backed down. He had second thoughts about leaving his large practice, and wondered whether he had the fortitude to start anew in a state he had visited only a couple of times and initially disliked. His first exposure had come as a physician for a Boy Scout jamboree in Santa Ana, and he could not imagine why anyone wanted to live in such a dusty place. A few years later, however, while teaching mouth-to-mouth resuscitation to emergency care providers in Orange County, he saw a different side of the area. He was particularly intrigued by a one-year-old amusement park called Disneyland, and decided that in the distant future he would retire there.

But after switching his original decision, Max changed his mind again, this time for good. The *Buffalo Courier-Express*—the paper that had *not* reported his arrest—ran a large article about the popular physician leaving town. He was feted throughout January with farewell parties. Attendees included grateful patients, high-ranking police and fire department representatives, even Boy Scout executives. Max was leaving Buffalo on a high note.

At one such party he was introduced to a 21-year-old man who asked if he could drive West with Max. The trip took three weeks; along the way they fell in love. They stayed together for five years. He was Max's first live-in partner, and he shared in the excitement as Max made a new, even more successful life for himself in notoriously conservative Orange County, Calif.

Clearly Max Schneider is not your average, run-of-the-mill gay physician. And he was not your average, run-of-the-mill boy either.

His story begins in the '20s in Buffalo, the industrial city where his father and grandfather were also born and raised. Over 70 years later Max still recalls his dreams as a 4-year-old; they were about men. For several years he fooled around with a slightly older cousin; that fulfilled his dreams. Like many teenage boys Max and his friends experimented sexually with each other. He enjoyed it immensely but knew he was expected to date girls. He did, yet he derived no pleasure from being with women. He preferred playing football, swimming, wrestling, boxing, and serving as editor of his high school newspaper.

His favorite activity, however, was scouting. With his troop at Temple Beth Zion, he earned the nickname "Mr. Boy Scout of Buffalo." He earned 67 merit badges, along with Eagle Scout rank, and never once did a leader come on to him. ("In high school a teacher did approach me," Max recalls. "I rebuked him. To this day I regret it!")

From the age of 10 Max knew he would follow in the footsteps of his hero, his family doctor. He appreciated the way the physician treated his mother, a chronically ill woman. Max bought a toy first-aid kit. One day after a fire down the block, Max offered to treat a fireman's cut. From that day on, his twin interests—medicine and working with emergency responders—were one.

Max entered the University of Buffalo (now the State University of New York at Buffalo) as a premed student. He also joined the cheer-leading squad. Then, on December 7, 1941, Japan bombed Pearl Harbor. The following day Max volunteered for the Army Air Corps.

Three months later he was called up and sent to basic preflight training in Vermont and Tennessee. At flight school in Georgia it was determined he lacked depth perception. His dreams of flying dashed, he became a radio operator. But he never lost sight of medical school.

On October 3, 1945, he was honorably discharged. The next day he was back in Buffalo for medical school. He was two weeks late and lacked the credits his classmates had.

Certain he was the only gay medical student in the world—as well as the only gay Jew—he debated seeing a psychiatrist. However, he was sure that would mean the end of medical school. Instead he convinced himself to give up "queerdom." So he butched his life up, slept with girls, and endured several months of torture.

Finally, after much anguish, he came to a new conclusion. "I told myself the most important thing about being a good doctor is integrity," he says. "And I knew that integrity begins within." So in 1946, at age 24 ("And quite a hunk," he says proudly), Max walked into his first gay bar.

It was "sleazy." But half a century later he remembers the decor less than the first face he saw. It belonged to a young Jewish man he knew as the brother of a classmate. "We both froze. Then we burst out laughing because we each knew why we were there," Max says. "Now I knew there were two gay Jews in the world. From that point on it was a gay life for me."

He graduated in the top fifth of his class and accepted a gastro-enterology fellowship at Harvard Medical School. He did well there, in between volunteering with the Boston Fire Department and going to gay bars.

Back in Buffalo, Max opened a private practice. He had no idea whether any family members or straight friends knew he was gay. He found out later that most—though not his parents—had figured it out by the time he was 15 but said nothing.

He flourished professionally and personally. His research on mouth-to-mouth resuscitation was exhilarating; so was his new interest in alcoholism, a field he entered after realizing that while many gastric diseases are alcohol-related, little research had been done on the subject.

Max's new practice in Orange County turned out to be as successful as his old one in Buffalo. His life was good too. He led a hospital Explorer post (affiliated with the Boy Scouts of America); he joined the faculty of the new medical school at the nearby University of California, Irvine; he earned recognition as the only doctor in the area doing addiction medicine.

Ironically, his lover discovered drugs, and after five years they broke up. But in 1969 Max met another man. They became a couple on June 20, 1970, and have been together ever since.

In those years Max has been named Orange County's "outstanding physician" and received the Golden Apple as UC Irvine's outstanding teacher. He is a founding member of both the Southern California and Bay Area chapters of Physicians for Human Rights. He has been named Man of the Year by the local gay and lesbian community center. He lectures on alcohol and addiction, and he consults frequently with fellow doctors on gay issues.

How has this openly gay physician led such a positive, fulfilling life, especially in two parts of the country that are not particularly gay-friendly?

Max explains: "It goes back to my first six months in medical school, when I figured out that to be a good doctor you must have integrity and be honest. Once I made that decision it was impossible to be ashamed of who I am. So I decided long ago that part of my philosophy of being a good doctor was to come out if necessary. I'm totally out in society, and it has never affected my practice. Not once. When I first came to California, I specifically asked a newspaper reporter to mention in a story about me that I am gay. To this day I continue to make sure it's included." Still, he gets butterflies every time he sees a story in print, and coming out remains a daily process, even for a 77-year-old. But, he reiterates, "Nothing bad has ever happened to me because I'm gay."

The reason for that, he says, is simple. "People want to do the right thing. Sometimes I think we don't give enough credit to doctors and patients for doing the right thing. People who don't know a gay person might fear or hate them, but once you're honest and forthright, the way I try to be, people react well."

He casts his memory back several decades to before World War I, when there was one word no one ever uttered in polite society. "That word was..." He pauses for effect. "*Cancer.* It was such a feared, deadly disease that no one could talk about it out loud. Well, that word has since come out of the closet.

"It's the same thing with 'gay.' People in Buffalo are no longer set up and arrested for being gay, as I was. And back then, the bars were sleazy. We needed my place in Canada to play croquet, knit, or do whatever we wanted. Now there are all kinds of social opportunities and organizations for every kind of gay person imaginable. We're out as a community."

And what does being gay mean at the start of a new millennium for a young man like he was 60 years ago, someone who enjoys helping people, loves medicine, and harbors the dream of being a doctor? "Most places it doesn't mean a tinker's damn," he says firmly. "Most medical schools are like the ones here in California. Today, we've got support systems in place for gay and lesbian students. It's perfectly fine to be exactly who you are. That's the best way I know to get to be a good doctor."

And with that forceful statement Max Schneider heads off. He and his partner of 30 years must clean their house. Three dozen gay and lesbian medical students are on their way over for a pool party.

"Noel": Airline Pilot

From the "mile-high club" and the movie *Airplane!* to ad campaigns in which stewardesses suggested "Fly me" and the stereotype that most male flight attendants are gay, the airline industry has a reputation as one in which sex is as available as an E-ticket and everyone, from the captain on down, comes a lot quicker than the average passenger's baggage.

That might be true for some people. But not Noel. He has been flying commercial planes for 10 years. He knows his coworkers—other pilots, flight attendants, even the ground crew—are having sex. "Most people screw around," he says matter-of-factly. "A layover is literally that. Those straight people go crazy." But for several reasons—his desire to separate his work from his personal life; his family and

43

religious upbringing; his natural reserve—Noel rarely goes out after landing in a new city. He never dates anyone in the industry. And it is incomprehensible to him that he would ever have a casual conversation—let alone a relationship—with a fellow gay pilot. In fact, Noel has never met another pilot that he knows for certain is gay.

For a decade that has been the reality of Noel's life, and he makes no apologies for it. "I don't need my work to provide a piece of ass," he says, with only a trace of his native Caribbean accent lilting his words. "I find that to be very, very sad. I have a full life outside of work, and that life is satisfying enough for me."

Although he works in a field in which fitting in, fitting an image, and fitting certain specific job requirements is of paramount importance, Noel has felt different in many ways for a long time. Born in the West Indies 30 years ago to parents of African, Portuguese, and English descent, he moved to Asia at age 8 when his father—a pilot—changed jobs. Noel considers that continent to be where he grew up.

Noel's father's job enabled him to travel often. He saw the world and explored different cultures. Travel was attractive, but Noel's father dissuaded him from following in his footsteps; being a pilot was too disruptive to family life, he argued. Noel was always very interested in health and nutrition, so he entered the University of Hawaii with thoughts of becoming a dietitian.

But one day during his junior year Noel took a flying lesson. He was hooked. He immediately understood that piloting a plane meant completing certain tasks in a certain order. There was a structure to everything—filing a flight plan, checking the cockpit, working the instruments for takeoffs and landings—that appealed to his task-oriented personality.

At the same time, flying made him feel comfortable. "I fit in simply because I was doing something well," he says. "I didn't realize it at the time, but because of my sexuality I had never fit in anywhere before. Now that I think about it, I can see that flying is not personality-driven at all. You're judged on one thing: how well you do your job. You don't have to reveal yourself in any way. That was fine for me. Flying made me feel very, very safe."

Noel's father was not pleased to learn of his son's love of flying nor of Noel's decision to leave college to attend flight school. He asked Noel to think things over for three weeks. Noel agreed. Exactly three weeks later he dropped out of college and signed up for flying lessons.

His first job was with a commuter airline. For three years he flew Caribbean routes. The first years of anyone's working life are difficult, especially in a profession as demanding as aviation, but Noel faced another challenge: He was in the middle of coming out.

For over a decade—ever since "figuring out" at age 10 or 11 that he was attracted to males—Noel had been fighting his homosexuality. He had girlfriends but felt no intimacy with them. Then at 22 he had his first same-sex experience. It was in the Caribbean, with an older man he had met in Los Angeles. "That was great," Noel recalls quietly. "He knew exactly how to deal with me. He was very considerate and respectful. Having that as my first experience—my model—has, I believe, kept me out of trouble ever since."

But Noel was hesitant to date in the Caribbean. "No matter where I was, it was too close to home," he explains. "Each island is separate and unique, but you take them all together and there is a very small-town mentality there." No matter which island he flew to, the only discussions he heard involving homosexuality were negative.

Pilots are well respected in the Caribbean, Noel says, which only added to his worries. He feared doing anything to sully either his profession or his reputation. To find dates he went all the way to Miami. "It was a very confusing time," he admits. "I had a girlfriend because I was still not sure about the gay thing, but I also had a boyfriend there."

In his mid 20s Noel was offered a promotion that would have required him to live in San Juan, Puerto Rico. He turned it down because he knew he had to leave the Caribbean. Although he yearned to grow professionally, he also felt a need to express himself sexually. Providentially, a week later he was offered the chance to be based on the U.S. West Coast. He accepted eagerly, and he traces both his sexual awakening and professional growth to that move. He rose through the ranks and now holds the rank of captain in the regional division of a major airline. He is in charge of his entire crew, which means taking full responsibility for all decisions. He is, he says happily, "head honcho whenever the plane is in the air."

But Noel was not always so confident. It took him until age 27 to come out to his family. With two older brothers (who are also pilots), he had heard few positive words about homosexuality. And he had always been the studious, religious sibling. Yet as he grew older, he realized that at the same time he was seeking a connection with God, his church was pushing him away. "Basically, I had no life," he says of his life through his mid 20s. "I promised myself I would find one."

But to Noel, having a life is not synonymous with having a job. "I don't think I ever thought about this before, but I realize now, my personality does not have to come out at all in the plane. If I don't choose to show it, I can be a boring or low-key pilot, but that does not mean I'm a bad one. If I had become a dietitian, I would have had to share a lot of myself with clients and customers. As a pilot I don't need to reveal anything of me to my passengers."

Or to his crew members. "At work I'm asexual," Noel says flatly. "A lot of pilots are ex-Navy, ex-military. Most of our conversations are about work, about flying. When the talk turns sexual, I join in. I grew up with two brothers, so I know how I'm supposed to talk. But I never reveal much. They just think I'm quiet. And because I look young they probably think I'm sexually inexperienced." Occasionally, when he flies with someone he thinks is particularly open-minded, Noel will talk about his sex life. But he never outs himself. Even with liberal copilots he always switches the gender of his partner from male to female.

How does all this make Noel feel? "It doesn't make me feel anything," he claims. "What I do feel is accomplished as a pilot. Flying is my job; it's not my life. It's fun, and it's a break from the rest of my life—from the stigma and prejudice I see and feel. It's a way to see God and look at nature from a different point of view. When I'm flying I can be quiet, I can meditate. It's almost a religious experience. It's a way to get away from my sexuality."

Noel, who calls the promiscuity of his colleagues "sick," sticks rigorously to his personal "no-sex" rule. "Lots of flight attendants are young. They see their job almost like they're still in college. And lots of pilots—even the married ones—are willing to oblige. I think that's sad. I've never been promiscuous to begin with, so that doesn't appeal to me. I just don't go out much on the road. I'm a strict vegan, so if people ask, I sometimes use that as an excuse."

Noel knows that not going out is odd for a pilot. "To me, I'm still in my work mode even after we land. And I'm very much a loner, so I don't have a great need to meet people or go dancing." But there is more to his reluctance to socialize. "It's too risky for me to go to a gay bar," he says. "All it would take is one guy to recognize you—maybe a member of the ground crew, who doesn't have anything to lose—and the word would spread like wildfire."

His fear, he says, is legitimate. He heard of a West Coast–based pilot who was outed. Everything was fine until the pilot traveled to a training center in another city for recertification. Such "check tests" are always conducted by one person, who has the power to pass or fail a pilot. "If he doesn't like you, he can always find a reason to flunk you," Noel says. "This guy was homophobic, and the pilot failed. The airline fired him, and once that's on your [Federal Aviation Administration] record you never work again. Essentially, one guy holds your career in his hands. Check pilots are FAA-certified and held in high esteem. Most of them are pretty cool, but no one asks whether they're homophobic or not. It's nothing that anyone talks about openly. I know it's a minute risk, and if I was doing my check rides here on the West Coast, I'm sure it would be OK. But both my father and brother have advised me not to come out, and considering everything, that sounds like pretty good advice."

Noel has firsthand experience with homophobia too. "About half the pilots are very vocally antigay," he says. "They tolerate the gay flight attendants because they have to work with them, but when they close the cockpit door I hear the other side of it. There are so many jokes and comments, it's incredible." He says that because he "understands the male ego" he does not find such talk threatening. (His colleagues complain about female pilots too, he notes.) "I actually join in the gay stuff. I talk about 'them.' But that's just because I divorce myself so much from my sexuality at work. It doesn't bother me, because I know my work life and my private life are two different things."

Noel has had one close call. Last year a flamboyant flight attendant saw Noel dancing at a gay bar. The pilot panicked—and then saw the same flight attendant a few days later at a gay beach. "I approached him and told him I'd prefer he not tell anyone," Noel recalls. "He said he wouldn't. We talk at work now, and he's become a good friend. He told a few flight attendants about me, and they're respectful. That impressed me. I didn't think they'd be like that." Noel believes the stereotype that many flight attendants are gay is accurate. He says the position attracts "compassionate, caring people who are expressive and understanding of others." And, he adds, "There is a lot of sex available. They can travel to White Parties all over the world."

The flight attendants have told Noel they have slept with half a dozen gay pilots, all based in his West Coast city. That eases his mind, but he has no plans to approach any of them—even just to be friends. He also has heard about a married pilot who was spotted at a gay gym and bathhouse. He "sort of" came on to Noel once. "I can't respect that," he says. "But I do feel sorry for him."

Noel downplays the popular perception of pilots as jaunty, thrill-seeking hero figures. "It doesn't take much to fly," he says. "You need two or three years' experience in basic skills. It appeals to people who don't want a 9-to-5 job; that's why a lot of military people come into the industry. Initially there is a definite thrill—your first flight is amazing—but not everyone keeps feeling that thrill. The ones who do are in tune with themselves. Some people get pretty negative about flying because there is a lot of company BS and boredom. I've seen some pretty miserable pilots. There are plenty of guys who bitch about being away from home so much too. I can't get into that. They knew what this job was about before they got into it."

Recently, since coming out to his family and earning his captain's wings, Noel's perspective has changed a bit. "I don't out myself in the

bods, sand dunes, and Dupont Circle are a long way
ive Oklahoma. And it was mere coincidence that he
he San Francisco Bay Area at exactly the same time the
movement was exploding all over the country.

wing up in Oklahoma, Dan did not deal with his sexual-
hose faraway Humboldt State University only because it
undergraduate oceanography program. When he arrived
ough, deep in California's lumber country, he realized he
g outdoors, not undersea. He changed his major to
ement and natural resources, graduating in 1975.

Humboldt State for many reasons: The setting was
lty members were supportive and accessible, and he
self in the school and its surroundings. "It was very lib-
n a place where no one has any expectations of who I
"I didn't know a soul when I got there. I could be
ted to be. I suppose I was closeted, because by then I
as gay, but it just wasn't an issue. I didn't date, but in
country at that time, marriage was frowned upon by
The only talk about 'the mold' was that no one should
it into it."

reputation as a liberal enclave, Humboldt lay behind
Curtain." There were no gay support groups. Had he
ly gay life, Dan would have had to travel 300 miles
ncisco—and there was no easy public transportation.
have been in Canada," he says. "So I guess things
as I thought. But because I wasn't dealing with being
't really affect me."

in college, Dan landed a summer job back in
Platt National Park (now part of the Chickasaw
ional Area). He performed classic ranger work—col-
gning campground sites, treating children who had
was hooked. His first full-time job after college was
the spectacular virgin redwood park a short distance
ncisco. His primary responsibility was interpreting:
s, assisting at the visitors center, and working with

cockpit, but now I am willing to say things like 'Hey, it works for them. They're valid people too.' Now that I'm captain I set the tone not to say anything negative about anyone. As an officer I couldn't do that."

The reaction, he says, is largely favorable. "Most pilots do see a lot of different people, they are friends with flight attendants, so they can say, 'OK, that's cool.' But I do it diplomatically. I don't throw a hissy fit." It helps, he says, that he sets a similar tone on racial matters. "Even though I look white, I am part black. So I draw strength from the idea that discrimination is discrimination wherever it occurs. I draw parallels, and I think a lot of people get it."

Noel assumes that his experience is typical. "I have never spoken to another gay pilot, so I have to assume most of them are like me. We keep our private lives private. I literally do not know any other gay male pilots other than rumors. I've heard stories, but I would never ask. Like I've said, I keep my private life private. That's just the way I am. My sexuality and my job are two different things."

Noel has come to terms with his homosexuality and appears to have made a clear distinction between it and his career. "I love what I do," he says fervently. "I adore the fact that I can see nature from the sky. I appreciate the benefits of traveling the world for free. Sometimes I fly two days a week and have five off. That's cool too, because I love my free time. The more senior you are, the more money you make and the less you fly. How can you beat that?"

He says he would change nothing about his work—including coming out. "My life would not change that much" if he was openly gay, he says. "Sure, I'd love the industry to be more open, accepting, and respectful, and less small-minded, but it's just not that big a deal."

DAN SEALY: PARK RANGER

As a chief ranger for the National Park Service, Dan Sealy enjoys nearly everything about his job. He loves researching and understanding complex ecological relationships and passing that knowledge on to park guests. He thrives on the diverse nature of his work, which ranges from finding lost hikers and patrolling campgrounds to protecting natural resources and fighting forest fires. He appreciates the dedication of his colleagues and supervisors, thousands of men and women who share his passion for the outdoors and our nation's heritage.

One thing Dan Sealy cannot stand, though, is sex in the sand dunes, bushes, and forests of the public land he loves.

As an openly gay man, that sometimes presents a conflict. He feels uncomfortable at Park Service meetings when the subject of

public sex—which, more often than not, in
bians, not straight people—comes up. Even
been chastised by members of the gay comm
know what business he (that is, the governm
for what they say is consensual sex in the pri
dunes, bushes, and forests.

"It's just not right," Dan says about pu
people have to clean up condoms and get ric
are scratched in trees. Park rangers have to
from these places. This is not an indictmen
indictment of public sex on government lanc
has a right to go. I don't like having to def
people should really be getting a room."

The National Park Service, Dan's employ
he says, a "mother and apple pie organiza
stituents—millions of park users each year—
ration. "They want Johnny Appleseed," Dan
giving an interpretive talk about nature or h

Nonetheless, Dan's sexuality has seldom b
work and has been for over 15 years. He has
the Park Service career ladder to his present
the way he has earned the respect of colleagu
rangers he has worked with across the countr
park users he has met.

Yet he remains one of the few gay people
Dan estimates the number of openly gay N
The percentage who are closeted, he says, is

Part of the reason for his acceptance may
has spent most of his career. At Muir Woo
and Marin Headlands he was just a few m
And when he transferred to the Cape Co
found himself by another gay paradise: Pro
he works near the NPS's national headquart
He has, he admits, been lucky to do work
feel isolated or ostracized doing it.

school groups. At Muir Woods, Dan also got his first taste of natural resource management (treating wildlife diseases and dealing with endangered species).

"It's weird," he recalls. "I'm not an airhead, but when I get wrapped up in something I can be completely unaware of whatever else is going on around me. This was in the middle of the whole *Tales of the City* era, but I had no idea San Francisco was a gay mecca." Throughout his entire time there he went to San Francisco only once.

Still not completely sure of his homosexuality, he returned to Oklahoma. His older brother, David, had recently come out, and Dan had seen the difficulty his parents experienced dealing with that. He did not want to hurt them further, so he remained closeted. (By the time Dan finally came out to his parents several years later, his father—a fireman, policeman, and warehouse worker on an Air Force base—and his mother, a housewife, were more knowledgeable about homosexuality and accepted the news with understanding and calm concern. They are now active PFLAG members. David, an architect, died several years ago of AIDS.)

In Oklahoma, Dan had a serious relationship with a woman, which might have led to marriage, had he not, in the back of his mind, known he was pretending to be someone he was not. His first same-sex experience was a one-night encounter with a man he met while hiking. Afterward Dan felt horrible. The reason, he says in retrospect, was because he suddenly realized he would not have the type of life he had always envisioned.

Dan spent two years working in various Oklahoma state parks. At the time they had no educational programs, making them "not much different from KOA campgrounds." The state parks director urged him to develop an educational program. More than 20 years later, Dan proudly notes, the project he designed continues to run strongly. Doing that work meant he moved often; that, he rationalized, was why he had no female relationships. Still, his one gay experience remained disturbingly vivid in his mind.

When he returned to Muir Woods as a temporary employee, he finally confronted his homosexuality. He had another one-night stand, this time with a Navy doctor. During the next few days Dan feared he would run into the man. He did not—but then he started wishing he would.

A coworker told Dan about a friend who took her to San Francisco gay bars. As they talked Dan took mental notes: "Castro! That's where gay people go!" One day he boarded a southbound bus. He was so naïve he did not realize that "the Castro" referred to an entire gay district. He asked the person next to him how to get there. The man opened his mouth and turned out to be "a flamboyant queen." He offered to take Dan there, then embarked on an anti–Anita Bryant tirade. The bus was filled with families. Dan shrunk down in his seat.

Over the next three months Dan made more forays into San Francisco. Each time he did nothing more than observe gay people in the Castro and on Polk Street. He noted the way they walked, talked, and danced. He was such a wallflower, Dan says, because he feared that if anyone found out who he was, he would be fired. He had never heard of the National Park Service terminating an employee for homosexuality, but he also did not know of anyone else at work who was gay. Being hired by the NPS had been his longtime goal. He would do nothing to jeopardize that.

A short while after Dan's second arrival at Muir Woods, openly gay San Francisco supervisor Harvey Milk and Mayor George Moscone were killed by a homophobic supervisor. In the visitors center, working with an elderly volunteer who reminded him of Katharine Hepburn, Dan listened on the radio as the new mayor, Dianne Feinstein, reacted emotionally to the assassinations. Something—to this day he cannot say what—compelled him to head to San Francisco. He made his way to City Hall, joining thousands of men and women holding candles in the dark. Milk's lover spoke, and Joan Baez sang. Both repeated Milk's mantra: Until every gay human being comes out of the closet, the world will not change.

Dan took this to heart and slowly began to come out. He joined Lavender Harmony, a gay and lesbian marching band. As often happens, he did not realize how public he was becoming about his homosexuality. One day—still not out at work—he called in sick and attended the gay pride festival. Lavender Harmony marched second in the enormous parade, right behind Dykes on Bikes. "There seemed to be a million cameras," Dan says. "And there I was, with my French horn and Hawaiian shirt."

No one said anything when he returned to work. His temporary park ranger job at Muir Woods became permanent. He came out to a female coworker but asked her not to tell anyone else. He wanted people to judge him for his work, not his sexuality. He designed excellent exhibits, found more than his share of lost children, and earned top ratings. His rapport with his supervisors was outstanding.

In 1980 he transferred to Marin Headlands, a ruggedly beautiful section of the Golden Gate National Recreation Area. His boss was "a classic ranger: kind-hearted, wise, always thinking of the park and the people using it, a good role model." Occasionally the issue of gay people arose; after all, the park was just across the bridge from San Francisco, and there was nudity on its beaches. Rangers who otherwise seemed nice made derogatory comments. His boss never did, but Dan, who by that time was living with a man and his two children, realized that keeping quiet at such times was a form of dishonesty. He made an appointment to have lunch with his boss.

His supervisor was not surprised to learn Dan was gay. In fact, he already knew: Someone had outed Dan two weeks earlier. Dan's boss told him the news had not stopped him from submitting Dan's name for an upcoming law enforcement training program. The boss said he had never suspected Dan was gay and that Dan's "non-flamboyance" had changed his perception about homosexuality.

Relieved, Dan came out to everyone. His openness enabled him to be much more relaxed at work. Outdoors, surrounded by beauty, reveling in the natural and cultural history that Park Service employees are expected to know, Dan was happier than he ever had been. And when tragedy struck—the home he shared with his lover and the man's children burned to the ground—his straight colleagues arrived with food and offers of housing. Through the difficult months ahead, their support never wavered.

In 1988 Dan transferred again—this time cross-country, to Cape Cod National Seashore. He was wiser than before but still a bit naïve. "I'd never been to Cape Cod," he says, laughing softly at the memory. "In my mind I imagined I was moving to a place like Maine. No one told me Provincetown is a huge gay resort!" In fact, Dan had randomly applied for work at the north district of the long, skinny park—landing smack in the middle of one of America's most active gay communities.

It was so active, in fact, that nudity was an even bigger issue than in California. In Provincetown, Park Service rangers and law enforcement agents regularly found and arrested gay men for public sex. Dan came out at work shortly after he arrived. He made his opposition to sex in the sand dunes known and, to his relief, never faced an awkward situation. He enjoyed his years on Cape Cod immensely.

Dan's current job is chief of the branch of Natural Resource Management at George Washington Memorial Parkway in suburban Washington, D.C. He says that since coming out at Marin Headlands, his Park Service experiences—as both a ranger and a supervisor—have been entirely positive. He pauses, though, and offers a clarification. For 20 years he has volunteered on a fire crew, and that is one place he remains in the closet.

"It's very hard work," he says. "You've got thousands of people— helicopter people, safety people, fire-fighting people—and in order to have any success everybody has to be on the same page. It's just like the military." It is like the military too in that the essential units are all small and self-contained. Composed of 20 men and women, these "hand crews" spend three weeks at a time doing backbreaking labor, battling an unpredictable enemy in dangerous, unfamiliar terrain. Whenever a fire breaks out, hand crews are formed randomly from a variety of government agencies. Members, who come from a variety of backgrounds, are expected to travel, work, eat, sleep, shower—and get along—together.

"Everyone absolutely has to support each other," Dan says. "People get banged up, they're dirty, they're sick, they're tired, and there are all kinds of personal dynamics going on. If someone is a jerk or making racist or homophobic remarks, you just sort of have to take it. You know you're going to be with them for the next three weeks, and everyone has to pull their own share. You learn to keep personal feelings out of it."

Dan has worked himself up to crew boss, though he prefers being a crew member—he calls it a nice change from his normal supervisory work. Fire crew work is so hard, he says, that sex is the last thing on his mind. Furthermore, he does not need the added distraction of dealing with crew members' fears. "Because I'm responsible for the safety of a lot of people, I choose not to bring my sexuality into the field," he explains. "I just don't want it to be an issue out there. We've got enough to do without worrying about gossip and innuendos and stereotypes."

During his normal workday at his Virginia office, Dan sees the National Park Service from a different perspective than he did in California and Cape Cod. The men and women who work for the agency are a cross-section of America—geographically speaking, at least. However, he notes, lack of racial diversity is an issue. Some members of minority groups believe the organization does not address its issues or concerns. The perception—inside the agency and out—is that the NPS is tradition-bound.

Dan disagrees. As President Clinton's Secretary of the Interior, Bruce Babbitt was adamant about including sexual orientation as part of the department's nondiscrimination policy. The move served notice to all NPS employees that they would have nothing to fear by coming out. "It didn't change the way I do my job," Dan says, "but now I know there are people here who are willing to help me, and I can help others. We can be open not just because we want to, and because it's the right thing to do, but because it's the law."

Though he loves his work, Dan admits there is one aspect he still does not understand. "Some people in the gay community have a weird fascination with people in uniforms," he says. That is why he seldom tells strangers what he does. "They've got all these stereotypes of park rangers. They make assumptions about my interests. They think I know everything about the outdoors, and nothing else, or that I'm a grown-up Boy Scout. Sometimes they make me feel like I'm one of the Village People. I want people to get to know me as a person, not a uniform."

So Dan Sealy introduces himself as an environmental scientist. "It bores them, and that's fine with me," he laughs.

"MATT": MASON

Bare Essence is a strip joint. Like many in mid Manhattan, it opens early. Sometimes in midwinter, when the temperature dips below freezing and cement cannot be mixed, the first customers are bricklayers from a nearby job site.

Stripping is a job, the same as masonry. It pays the bills, it requires a certain skill, and the longer you do it, the more you learn. "Matt," a mason, has become quite good at his job. He knows precisely where to place his tools for maximum efficiency, how to choose the right brick every time, and exactly how a finished row should feel when he runs his hand over it. A good stripper is equally adept at judging her audience. She senses what each man wants, then makes sure he gets it.

One Bare Essence stripper was particularly astute. Something in Matt's manner—maybe the way his eyes roamed differently from other men's or the fact that he never licked his lips when she took off her pasties—told her that Matt was not particularly interested in her morning performances.

She was not offended; after all, stripping was her job, not her life. So she decided to have a little fun with Matt—she figured he would not mind. She made certain she paid particular attention to him; she saved her most seductive lap dances for him and pretended the two of them shared the sexiest chemistry of everyone in the dingy joint.

She sensed Matt's secret, and the ruse worked. Whenever the stripper shook her stuff on the bar top, just inches from 24-year-old Matt's face, the older masons went wild. "Oh, to be young again!" they hooted.

If they only knew, Matt thought to himself. *If they only knew.*

Matt himself did not know until he was in high school. Before that, in junior high, he fooled around with girls. Even when Matt was 13 and one of his three older brothers came out, alarm bells never rang. His entire family had always assumed his brother was gay. Matt's only problem with that was a reluctance to bring friends to the house. He never imagined he might be gay too.

Like many Brooklyn boys, Matt played school-yard sports. He also loved skateboarding and was good at it: In the early '90s his picture appeared several times in *Thrasher* magazine. But when he was 16 skateboarding's appeal faded; the new thrill became raves. Several nights a week, one side of the Limelight was gay. Matt grew curious and befriended a group of bisexual club kids. "Before I knew it situations started happening," he says obliquely. "Suddenly everything made sense."

His family moved to Staten Island, but every Friday night he left for the clubs, then slept at a friend's house back in Brooklyn. When he returned Monday morning his parents had no idea where he had been, what he had done, or who he hung out with.

But you can't be a club kid forever, and when he graduated from high school Matt needed a job. He worked for two years as a carpenter's helper, building half-pipes and skate ramps. A few years later, needing more money, he decided to become a mason. He knew that union bricklayers earn good wages, that every job is different, and that at the end of the day a mason can step back, survey his work, and take pride in what he has accomplished. Matt also knew that bricklaying is "a very masculine job."

Every work shanty—the trailer where masons store their tools, eat breakfast, talk sports, and change into work clothes—is plastered with photographs of naked women. However, as in many male-dominated workplaces, there is also an underlying homoerotic dynamic. In the shanty, behind closed doors, men swish, lisp, and "act gay"—all, of course, in jest. "That's the perfect time for me to do a bad impression of a gay person or grab someone's nipples," Matt says. "I don't get off on that. I'm just, I guess, portraying part of the attitude of the rest of the guys. We're all trying to impress each other with how macho we are."

Matt is completely closeted at work. Although he has had a lover for over five years, not one of his fellow bricklayers knows. Statements like "Christ, my broad kept me up the whole friggin' night" are the closest Matt comes to divulging details of his personal life.

"A typical job lasts six or 12 months. After that I'll probably never see those guys again," he explains. "I don't need to share stuff with people like that. Besides, even though bricklayers work together, it's not like we're partners. Everyone has their own 10 feet of space. I've never had a situation where I came out on the job, and I can't imagine one where I would."

In addition, he notes, "this is a very old trade. Eighty percent of the guys are old-timers getting ready to retire. Some of them come from Italy. There's no way in hell the topic of homosexuality could ever come up with them. And now we've got a lot of Jamaicans coming in. They think homosexuality is just about the worst thing in the world. I can't even think of having a discussion about it with them."

Yet lately Matt's closet door has inched open. For example, he put a pride sticker on his car. "When I drove to work in Brooklyn, I'd park at the far end, and I'd back in to the space so no one would see," he says. "But then again, I didn't rip it off just because I had a new work site to drive to."

The bricklaying trade, once exclusively male, has started to attract women. Matt estimates that 90% are lesbians. He finds common ground with some. They never quite come out to each other—communication is more by facial expressions and body language than words—but, like the stripper, the women sense his secret. Because most lesbian masons are not out either, they and Matt form a mutual protection society.

Matt draws a clear line between his work and his personal life. He can talk the talk with his colleagues—primarily about sports and getting drunk—but when they ask Matt to hang out with them, he usually begs off, saying, "I have a serious girlfriend, and I don't screw around anymore." Once in a while he will join them for a beer, pool, and darts, but he is always thankful the work day ends at 2:30 P.M. "It's not like that's the time to go pick up girls," he says with relief. "Mostly, when the whistle blows I'm the first guy to run off the site."

In recent months Matt has moved away from day work. His union elected him shop steward, so now his days are filled with administrative chores. Yet in union meetings, as on his job sites, the topic of homosexuality never arises. "We hear a lot of sexual harassment issues involving women, and there's pressure to be more respectful there," he says. "But I've never heard a word about anything like domestic-partner benefits. And I'm sure as hell not going to be the one to raise my hand and ask."

A major reason for Matt's adamant stance is the fear that if he ever came out or was outed and then tried to go back to work on a site, he would be blackballed for new work. When a job ends, masons call the union hall and wait for their next assignment. It usually took two or three days for Matt to receive a new job. However, he has seen colleagues who ran afoul of union rules—by working a side job for cash, for instance—wait two or three months before being called.

That is a risk Matt is unwilling to take. He enjoys his union activities but knows that one day his love for bricklaying will lure him back to the work shanty (hopefully, one far away from the Bare Essence strip joint). "Guys always tell me I do all the detail work well," he says proudly. "I'm the one they call to make sure the arches look right. I always want it to be perfect, even the places no one sees. I guess that's just the gay man in me."

DAVID GLASGOW: CHRISTIAN-BOOKSTORE CLERK

It's not unusual for a customer to walk into the Christian Publications bookstore in Camp Hill, Pa., and ask for a book to help them deal with the news that a spouse, relative, or friend has just come out as gay. After all, the 10,000-square-foot store is filled with material designed to help men and women—most of them religious conservatives—discover what God says about the weighty issues of the world.

What is unusual is the response they receive if the clerk they ask is David Glasgow. The 29-year-old is apt to recommend *Is the Homosexual My Neighbor?*—hardly radical, but liberal enough that his store does not stock it. David thinks it is the best choice for such customers, however, and always offers to order it for them.

What is even more unusual is the reason David knows this is the best book for Christians hoping to learn more about homosexuality: He himself is gay.

If it seems unusual for a gay man to earn his living working in a Christian bookstore, it is. All day long David stocks shelves with publications that proclaim his sexuality to be wrong, even perverse. He rings up books with pages that promise, with God's will and much prayer, he can change. Even the CDs and cassettes he sells in the music department carry the message that homosexuals—and, by implication, David himself—are abnormal.

David is out to a few of his managers. Talk about perverse: One solution a Christian-bookstore supervisor proposed was to lie.

It is, David admits, an odd situation. But it is not untenable. He considers himself to be a good Christian. He likes his job, as well as (for the most part) his colleagues and customers. And he and his supervisors know he is an excellent employee.

Homosexuality makes up only one part of David Glasgow. It is an important facet of his life, but it is not everything.

Growing up in Columbia, Md., he inherited both his social liberalism and religious conservatism from his parents. His father—formerly a researcher at the National Institutes of Health, now a college professor of psychology—was raised a Southern Baptist. His mother, a teacher, had been a Roman Catholic. The family, however, became United Methodists. His church taught David that while it is not immoral to be gay, there are immoral ways to be gay (and straight). "I guess that's a brainy way of looking at religion," he says. "If something doesn't make sense, it's probably not true. I don't think God puts things on earth just to trick us."

Dickinson College, in Carlisle, Pa., is not a religious institution, but as a student there David joined a campus chapel group. A music composition and theory major, he also directed the high school–age choir at a nearby church. His positive impression of that church was reinforced when he sought counsel from a young associate pastor after a sexual escapade he was not particularly proud of. The clergyman replied that although he did not understand homosexuality, he

knew God loved, and would continue to love, David. That response
helped David come out at the end of his senior year during a concert,
by singing a song he wrote with a woman he calls his "Will &
Grace–type friend." His parents had learned of his homosexuality a
few months earlier after reading his mail. Just like his college friends,
they reacted with support. That gave him the courage to be a bit
more open.

Coming out also enabled him to meet the boyfriend with whom
he went shopping in 1995, two years after graduation. The couple
wandered into Christian Publications. Because David loves to read,
and the store also had a large music department—and because David
had just left a job waiting tables—his boyfriend urged him to apply
for a position. David expected to stay through the Christmas season.
Six years later he still works there.

The store is run by the Christian and Missionary Alliance, a
denomination dedicated to overseas mission work. In addition to the
book, Christian music, and gift departments, the building contains a
publishing house. The store workers tend to be less conservative and
traditional than the publishing staff. Still, says David, his homosexuality has rarely come up. That is fine with him.

"Most people know implicitly that I'm gay," he says. "They
understand that my boyfriend and I share more than a room—we've
got a mortgage." He thinks one reason his homosexuality is not discussed, or even acknowledged, is that it creates cognitive dissonance
in his avowedly Christian colleagues. "They say to themselves—at
some level, not necessarily consciously—'Dave is one of *them*, but
he's also one of us. Now, wait a minute: What does that say about
him and us?'

"I tend to believe that truth will always win out. I'm not any less
Christian because I'm gay, and I'm not any less gay because I'm
Christian. I think that's something other people in the store are
dealing with too. They just have to figure it out their own way, at
their own pace."

David has been heartened by small gestures. For instance, an elderly woman who had worked at the store "since the time of Jesus"

said each night before she left, "Say hi to Mark for me." David notes, "She didn't have to say anything more. I knew what she meant."

There are several degrees of homosexuality in the Christian world, David says. "Open homosexuals" are particularly troublesome. One day an assistant manager told his boss that David was openly homosexual. The supervisor brought him in, told him he should not be "open," and suggested that if anyone asked David if he was gay, he should lie. (This same supervisor also told David that he was one of the store's three best workers in 25 years.)

"I couldn't believe he said that," David marvels, nearly two years later. "This is a Christian bookstore!"

Fortunately, David has not had to decide whether to take that un-Christian advice, because no one has ever asked. If someone does, though, he says he will not lie. Dishonesty and shame are no longer parts of his life.

The hypocrisy of being directed to lie is not lost on the gay employee. "I'm used to that kind of thing," he says. "Evangelical Christians tend to be asexual. They have a chronic cheerfulness about certain parts of their lives. A lot of them have a tenuous grip on reality. When I show them the 'truth of life'—that I can live happily and healthily—it can be an affront to them. Well, Jesus showed people the truth of life too—at least in the Bible I read."

Whatever stress he feels at work, David says, comes not from dealing with antigay attitudes but from not having enough time to do everything. "That's universal," he acknowledges. "It's why we call it 'work.'"

Whenever a customer or colleague rants about "queers" or "those people," David keeps quiet. However, he says, his body language and facial expressions convey his confident disagreement. "The fact that I don't consider it a valid scriptural position makes them pause. And if they don't believe as I do, at least they start to realize there may be another valid point of view out there."

As noted earlier, he will speak up when a customer specifically requests a book on homosexuality. He knows that recommending a publication not regularly stocked puts him in a delicate situation.

But it is worth his career to tell parents their child will not go straight to hell simply because that child is gay.

David recognizes that his quiet attitude affects people. His assistant manager eventually apologized for bringing David's homosexuality to their boss. She said she had known about him for a long time and eventually realized that not only had it not affected their work relationship, but over time it had actually helped her understand a different viewpoint.

David, in turn, has been affected by his six years in a Christian bookstore. After reading about self-loathing gays and the "ex-gay" movement, he has felt the need to define who he is, and what being gay means, on his own. He believes that the answers about his life lie not on printed pages but within himself. "Being surrounded by the 'Christian viewpoint' has made me examine myself, my life, and my relationship with Mark in much greater detail than I probably would have," he admits.

David knows too that he is not the only gay man working in a Christian bookstore. In his six years he has met several other gays in the company, though all were much less comfortable with their sexuality than he is with his. One man tried to kill himself in David's kitchen on Palm Sunday. "Working in that environment can really create feelings of self-hatred if you're not entirely comfortable with who you are," he says. "I think for these other gay people their religion was very important, and they wanted to live out their calling. They thought their calling excluded their sexuality. For them, the truth of the Gospel was supposed to override everything else. One guy was even ready to get married to a woman he was not attracted to at all. I can't identify with denying everything I feel. I just wasn't raised that way. That's the kind of desperation that makes you grab a pair of kitchen shears and go for your throat."

A year ago David left the Methodist Church. He joined a Metropolitan Community Church congregation in Harrisburg, 20 miles away. Fortunately, that did not present a problem at the Christian bookstore; after all, he still attends services. It helps that most colleagues don't know that the MCC is a predominantly gay denomination. "I describe it as a church where diversity is very important," Dave says wryly. "The ones who know turn a blind eye."

Slowly but surely, David sees even the conservative Christian world changing. "I think more people are becoming convinced that a broad spectrum of sexuality is normal," he says. "Institutions change slower than individuals, but it's individuals who change institutions. Christian bookstores may not have gay-friendly hiring policies in my lifetime, but they may hire more gay people. It gives me a small measure of hope that those of us in a position to make small changes will be able to do that. And the ripples will spread from there."

All the way, perhaps, to the day when *every* clerk at Camp Hill's Christian Publications will be willing and able to direct any customer to a copy of a gay-positive book like *Is the Homosexual My Neighbor?*

"John": Apple Grower

You won't find Illinois atop the list of great apple-growing states. And rural Illinois is not exactly fertile hunting ground for a gay man. But, given the choice between taking over his family orchard or moving to a big city—Chicago, or even Peoria—in search of a husband, "John" chose apples.

It is a decision he once gladly made. Now, that choice causes him incalculable anguish.

The orchard was his father's idea 30 years ago, when he sought a way for his five children to work together. They did, until in the late '80s John's mother died of cancer. She was the family's emotional hub, and with that connection cut, John's siblings scattered. Some had never liked apple-growing at all; others realized they could not make a living at it. John, who planted his first trees at age 10, remained and began the long process of purchasing the orchard from his father. In retrospect, John says, he was looking for a way to gain approval from a man he had always tried to please but never could.

John was not a mama's boy, and when he realized at 14 that he was attracted to males, he vowed to hide that fact from the world by acting stoic and manly. Still, earning his father's respect was difficult. John was raised in a fundamentalist Christian home; he always understood homosexuality to be an evil choice. He is proud that as a young man he did not surrender to his same-sex temptations. "That shows I'm a strong person," he says. "I guess that's just the farmer in me."

He has, however, met people who came out when they were young and did not suffer for it. He admires their courage but cannot reconcile their actions with what he has been taught or what he sees in his corner of the world today. If he had a gay son, he says, he would advise him to stay in the closet. John explains, "I'd be sad for him because of what he'd have to endure."

John talks about his sexuality with great reluctance. He speaks quietly, almost embarrassedly, about the recent breakup of a seven-year relationship and his difficulties reconciling his homosexuality with his Christianity. Mention apples, though, and John cannot keep still.

"Owning an orchard is fascinating," he says, relieved to be moving on to a more comfortable subject. "It's the only occupation I know where one person takes a product and handles it from the beginning right to the very end. You plant it, you spray it, you prune it, you grow it, you market it, and you sell it to the final consumer. Even a farmer who grows other crops ends up selling to a co-op or storage elevator. But with apples, you're the only one."

John loves watching customers—especially children—pick their own apples at his orchard. They also pick pumpkins, raspberries, sweet corn, and Christmas trees. John has diversified, both to avoid a complete crop failure and because—it breaks his heart to say this— apples don't sell nearly as well as they used to. "People these days eat one a week," he laments. "It's true that an apple a day keeps the doctor away, but Americans don't believe it anymore. They don't even appreciate the flavor. You know what's the most popular apple today? Red Delicious. That's so bland!"

When he realized that an entire generation of fresh apple pie bakers had died off, John provided ready-to-bake pies. "But some people don't even want that," he says with despair. "They'd rather buy a frozen apple pie in the supermarket. Do you have any idea how stale those taste?"

To combat his drop in sales, John also sells cider products—cider doughnuts, for example, and cider ice cream. Even so, he has had to downsize his orchard from 25 acres to 10. Coupled with his almost complete lack of gay life, it is clear why John feels depressed.

His corner of Illinois is dotted with small villages and towns. The few gay men he knows are closeted. In a community that lives and breathes by the rhythm of families, John often feels quite lonely.

"I dreamed once of moving to a city and living free," he admits. "But I never did. The orchard held me down. My roots are here. I wanted to be a good son—especially once I knew I was gay. I thought, *If I can prove to my family that I'm 'normal,' then I'll finally get their support and love.*"

It never happened. "They won't throw me out on the street. But because I'm gay, I know they don't want me to be very successful. They haven't given me a lot of help. I always feel like I'm out here, doing whatever I'm doing, all alone."

To combat his isolation John goes online. Yet even that experience can be fraught with danger. One incident in particular petrified him. "As you probably guessed, apples are my life. I have apples on my shutters and carved into my window boxes. I painted my house red. Everyone around here calls this the Apple House. Well, one day I was on AOL, and an Instant Message popped up. 'You live in the Apple House,' it said. I acted dumb. 'The one on the corner. You have an orchard,' the message said. I wanted to know who the guy was. He said a friend told him I was gay. I IM'ed him back that his friend was wrong. He said, 'No, I saw you go into your house with a man.' I got off my computer as quick as I could. I was terrified someone knew I was gay."

In fact, John often entered his house with a man—for seven years he shared his home with a lover. But John was so closeted that he made sure they had different phone numbers. They even had different addresses: One man used an RFD route, the other a street name. John admits that is sad, but he says it is the way things had to be.

"I'm blessed to not appear gay," John continues. "I'm very straight-appearing. I could never have survived in this area if people knew I was gay. I know that's tragic, but it's true."

John believes that if he came out publicly as a gay man, his business would shrivel and die like bad fruit. Straight people would not patronize a "gay orchard," he says, and he cannot imagine surviving on the few "queens" who would take their place. "I think in this area people think gays are a threat to the family," he says. "They think we recruit and abuse children. My billboard says, 'Bring your family to my orchard.' If they knew about me, that billboard would be seen as recruitment. I'm not worried about physical abuse, but I am worried about my business."

He calls his social life "lame." His former lover was seven years younger but much more in control. "He had all the experience," John says. "I was the virgin."

Yet despite John's fears, he is not completely closeted. His employees know he is gay, and nothing untoward has ever occurred. "I guess everything I imagined never happened," John says. He pauses as a new thought forms in his head. "Maybe I've been imagining a lot of things."

As he ponders his words, John realizes that he did appear in public with his boyfriend, and no one ever said a word or pointed a finger. "I guess I'm just very lost and unsure of myself," he concludes.

John recognizes that his life today is at a crossroads. Single again, he is right back where he was seven years ago. After voicing his thoughts about work and life for the first time, he begins to believe he can become more open—not only at his orchard but within his community. "Life is short," he says, mulling the concept out loud. "People might not react the way I fear."

Suddenly, he looks to the future. "My dream has always been to help young people who are struggling with their identity. I haven't done that yet, but I should. When I was a kid I never had anyone to talk to, and I know people need that around here. The guy who IM'ed me—he was a high school student. I found that out later, when I looked at his profile. He was probably struggling too."

But just as suddenly, John retreats. "The way he said 'My friend told me you were gay,' that was wrong. I couldn't come out to just anyone." For the third time in minutes John veers in a new direction. "Maybe if he IM'ed me today, I'd do things different." His voice tails off, woefully wistful.

Not quite 40, John looks at his life with a great deal of regret. His orchard lies miles from any major city. His trees are growing old. He lacks the capital needed to put his ice cream in stores. He answers the obvious question—*If you could do it all over again, would you?*—head-on, without wincing.

"Never. This area is pathetic. If I hadn't bought this orchard, my life would have been completely different. But I still would have struggled. And if I came out when I should have, in the late '70s, early '80s, I might've been subjected to AIDS and that whole thing, so I might not even be alive—but…" He pauses, collecting a bushelful of random, conflicting thoughts. "Listen. I love apples. I even sign my name with an apple. But sometimes I feel I've become like a mascot or a clown with this cause. People know me by my apples, but no one really knows who I am.

"I was a total nonperson in high school. I can't even imagine the things I missed. It's pretty sad when a man can't be who he is. So I guess I'm at a loss. The thing I've invested in—this orchard for 25 years—is going. I love this business because it makes me feel special and worthwhile, but to do this for the rest of my life…I don't know. I just don't know.

"And yet on the other hand, it's hard for me to support the gay lifestyle because it seems so destructive. To me, it's just not positive. There's just a lot of promiscuous, unsafe sex. I can't throw myself into that."

Finally, just as abruptly, John's mood turns again. "I am happy," he says, and his emotion seems genuine. "I am blessed. My friends are good ones. And this summer, when the weather turns warm, I think I'll work on my relationships. I know I can't spread myself too thin, because I care about my orchard, and I know I have to spend time at it. But sometimes I haven't taken time for the other things in life that are important, and now I have to make time."

He pauses for a long time, then utters one final thought. "I guess all of life is just one big balancing act."

RANDY BROWN, "ROD," VICTOR EMOVI: TRUCK DRIVERS

Randy Brown

When he got out of drug and alcohol rehabilitation in the mid '80s, Randy Brown needed a job. And he had to get away from cute guys; after all, he thought, trying to fight his gay impulses had driven him to drugs and alcohol in the first place. He already had his truck driver's license, so he signed on with a hazardous-waste hauling company.

The rig they assigned him was nothing like the small trucks he'd driven before. Randy peered up at a huge Peterbilt semi and instantly realized he was out of his league. He walked into the garage and announced he needed a little help. A coworker asked what he needed to know.

"Well," Randy said, "how do you get in?"

The man showed him. Randy climbed aboard. Suddenly he felt a surge greater than any drug he had ever taken.

Wow! he thought to himself. *I'm a truck driver! I am somebody! From now on I don't have to be a fag.*

Fifteen years later, Randy looks back and laughs. "I might as well have been a drag queen sitting up there in that big cab."

Driving a Peterbilt does not make a man any less gay than he already is. That is one of the many lessons Randy learned hauling steel, gasoline, and hazardous cargo in flatbeds, rolloffs, and tankers all across America.

He has heard the chatter about "good buddies." (Despite how it's used in popular culture, that CB term refers not to pals but to homosexuals.) He has learned that hustlers prowl rest stops, offering quick blow jobs to horny truckers of all sexual orientations. "There seem to be more gay truck drivers than I ever imagined," says Randy, who spent years in the closet before finally coming out, both at work and to his deeply religious family, with positive results. "We're not a majority, but we definitely are everywhere."

Most people would not use "gay" and "truck driver" in the same sentence. After all, truckers hardly fit the traditional image of gay men. "We spend a lot of time on the road," he acknowledges. "Viewed from the outside, we probably look and act seedy. The average worker, even the blue-collar guy, spends eight hours on the job then goes home. Truckers eat greasy food at greasy truck stops. We can't shower when we want. We don't need to wear wing tips or comb our hair for customers, so our personal hygiene suffers." Therefore, truck driving is hardly conducive to pursuing romance.

That's OK. For years romance was the furthest thing from Randy's mind. He grew up in Flat Rock, Mich., a semirural town of 7,000 south of Detroit where athletes reigned. Randy, who did not care for sports, turned to drinking and drugs, in part to obliterate his strong same-sex attractions. At 16 he and a friend often slept in each other's homes. As they feigned sleep, Randy says, "things happened. It was undeniable, but we denied it pretty well."

He told another boy, his best friend, that he thought he was gay. "The biggest news of the century in Flat Rock" raced through school, and he lost his best friend. Randy had no one to console or comfort him, no one to assure him he was normal. He lived for years with a broken heart. He did not permit himself to get close to anyone. He wanted to make sure that experience never happened again.

The word around Flat Rock was that Randy—all 6 feet, 180 pounds of him—was a sissy. A boy in history class called him a "stupid motherfucking faggot," then broke his nose. Randy, who did not want to be gay, suddenly found plenty of opportunities to have gay sex. "All the football players said they were drunk, but they probably passed the word around that Randy gives really good head," he says. Meanwhile, the one-time honor student's GPA plummeted to 1.5.

Randy always knew that after high school a job was waiting in his family's construction company. He joined right after graduation and worked there seven years. But the recession of the early '80s took its toll, and the business went under. All along, Randy had been growing apart from most human beings.

The process began at home. When Randy came out in his late teens to his mother, a church organist, she warned him never to tell his father, a liturgist who was studying to be an assistant pastor. Randy's younger brother already knew he was gay because Randy was having sex with his friends. In his early 20s Randy found a 16-year-old boyfriend. They worked together, spent all their time together, even slept together in Randy's parents' house (though no one ever talked about it). Yet Randy was as unhappy as ever.

He tried to change by having sex with women. Not once, however, did he desire them. "I might as well have been thinking about a piece of paneling," he says matter-of-factly. "The difference was, it's hard, and I wasn't." The more he thought about sex with men—but without "being gay," which in his mind signified physical, emotional, and spiritual pain—the more drugs and alcohol he consumed.

Finally, Randy checked himself into rehab. When he emerged

sober and found the hazardous-waste trucking job, his life turned around. Or so he thought.

"I realized, *I can get away! I don't have to be stuck in Flat Rock all my life!*" he says. "Of course, no matter where I went, there I was. I was still always a gay guy with a chance of getting his nose broken the second anyone knew." Though his job took him far beyond Flat Rock, he learned little about gay culture. He had not yet seen a gay magazine, not even a mainstream publication like *The Advocate*. The only other openly gay man he knew—"the town fag"—took him to a bathhouse in Detroit. Randy found it repulsive.

His fellow truckers did not make it easy to come out. Truck drivers, Randy says, are "big, tough, butch, macho, I'll-break-your-nose guys." The profession attracts emotionally insecure men, he believes, because being at the helm of an enormous machine gives them feelings of power and control. No matter how small a man is, Randy explains, driving a truck makes him feel big.

He calls the average intelligence level of most truckers "significantly below" that of other trades. Certainly, truck driving does require thinking—common sense is imperative—but Randy describes most of his colleagues as poorly educated.

As he traveled cross-country, Randy had occasional flings with local men. Some people at work knew he was gay; a coworker once discovered gay porn in Randy's glove compartment. For years thereafter, wherever he worked, the whispers followed. That was one more reason Randy never got close to his colleagues.

Then, on October 18, 1996, his life changed forever. That day, out of the blue, his father—a man who by then tacitly acknowledged his son's homosexuality but never seemed to accept it—called Randy. He said he had joined a group called PFLAG. In fact, he continued, he had been attending meetings for a while and was finally able to say the words "I am the proud parent of a gay son."

"Fuck you," Randy replied. "I don't believe it."

It was an instinctive response. Randy instantly recalled all the years he had been hurt; this, he thought, was just one more cruel trick. But when his father invited him to the next meeting, Randy cried for hours. It was the turning point of his life. No longer did he feel like "a sick faggot." For the first time he realized he could be completely, openly, honestly gay.

That meant he did not have to travel all over the country, attempting to run away from himself. Today, Randy drives trucks for a scrap metal hauling company in suburban Detroit. He is, he says, "way out." He did not plan things that way, but, like much of his life, things are now working out for the best.

He came out while serving as a safety team captain when a coworker made an antigay comment. Randy asked why the man always picked on people. "Faggots don't count," the colleague said. "And they don't work here, that's for sure."

A bolt of energy—as strong as the one he felt when sitting in his first Peterbilt cab but from a far different source—roared through Randy. "You just don't know, do you?" he erupted. "I'm sick and tired of you motherfuckers. I'm gay, and that's who I am!" At that moment he did not care if he lost his job or even his career. But he had enough sense to walk out of the room to keep from slugging the man.

He had barely reached the hall when most of the safety team emerged. "I'm so impressed!" the business agent said. "That took a lot of balls. We respect you. Please don't leave."

The staunch support stunned and impressed Randy. He understood, though, what would come next. Every trucker has a CB radio. He knew that, even faster than in high school, the word would spread throughout the industry: *Randy Brown is gay.*

Randy had trained many drivers. All, he imagined, would think the same thing: "Oh, my God. I spend time in the cab with a fag!"

Most of the men did think that. But they also had other thoughts: "I never would have known, so what's the difference?" "He never came on to me." "I don't want anyone prying into my personal life, so why should I give two shits about his?" As his colleagues shared their reactions with him, Randy seized the opportunity to educate them about the differences between gay men, predators, and pedophiles. Slowly the barriers between he and his colleagues dissolved.

His new relationships paid off when a coworker who did not

appreciate Randy's announcement began harassing him. Much of the gay bashing was verbal; occasionally, however, the man sabotaged Randy's equipment. Randy is not the type to run to management, but a fellow trucker with a gay relative passed the word. A superior asked Randy why he had remained quiet, then told him, "We'll do something. You are extremely valuable to us. We'd rather have you here than him." The company followed up with a strong memo vowing to prosecute any employee found guilty of sexual harassment.

Randy is proud that his company stands behind him but believes part of the reason is because he is a very good worker. He does not think they would take a stand for "just any gay person." Yet in the same breath he notes that the Teamsters union supports gay and lesbian rights. That means a great deal to him. It helps him be more comfortable with who he is. Not having to lie has made an enormous difference in his life.

Telling the truth has allowed Randy to relax about being a gay truck driver. He laughs as he describes arriving late for a meeting celebrating an anniversary of his sobriety. The only way to get there was in his truck. As he pulled into the parking lot, the members of his support group—all gay—gasped in awe. One man cooed, "You're so butch!" Another asked for a ride. A lesbian cracked, "That's our job!"

"It was such a stereotypical role reversal," Randy says. "But for the first time in my life I wasn't worried about what people might think."

Finally Randy Brown is at peace with himself. He is no longer promiscuous. Still, his newfound serenity allows him one last look backward.

"There are a lot of cute guys at work, and God knows I'd love to do them. But I know I have their respect, and right now that's the most important thing in the world to me."

"Rod"

Another truck driver who looks with amazement at his younger self is "Rod." When he began driving a semi out of a Pensacola, Fla., warehouse in 1982, he was 20 years old. Traveling cross-country, he heard other drivers talk about behind-the-scenes (more accurately, back-of-the-cab) action at truck stops, and he saw holes drilled in shower walls. Occasionally as he walked into a bathroom he would see two men hastily separate. But, he says ruefully, "I was not clued in. I had no idea what was happening. I knew nothing at all."

It was not that Rod was dumb. He just had grown up on a Pennsylvania dairy farm; in his small, sheltered, and very religious town and high school, he had little exposure to diversity. Finding himself at an early age sexually attracted to boys—and believing he was the only one with such feelings—he knew he had to leave as soon as possible. "People think of small towns as nice, friendly places, and maybe they are. But if you don't fit the mold, they're very oppressive and hateful," he says.

Within two days of graduation Rod packed his car and was gone. On a whim he enrolled in an electronics technical school in Phoenix. After six months, though, he realized it was not for him. He answered a newspaper ad for a cleaning supplies traveling salesman. That was not a good fit either. But the owner, who lived in Pensacola, needed a private chauffeur. For two years Rod filled that role. On the side he kept his employer's fleet of cars running well. When the company started hiring long-haul truck drivers, he applied.

With time to kill between deliveries and pickups, Rod searched out bookstores—real ones, not the XXX kind. Always a voracious reader, he surprised himself by researching homosexuality. He learned that it was not wrong, and he slowly began to accept himself as gay.

As his mind and heart opened up, so did his eyes. Rod learned he could meet like-minded men on the road. He enjoyed fooling around with them but hesitated to move past fondling. He was paranoid about being caught, either by the police or other truckers.

Many long-haul truckers have an odd double standard about homosexuality, he says. They make "fag jokes" with regularity but feel no compunction about engaging in sex with other men. They justify their actions many ways: "I'm on the road so long, away from my wife"; "This isn't real sex, just physical relief"; "I'm not gay, just messing around."

Rod, however, knows he is gay. A natural conversationalist, he tried to ask partners about their lives. Most said they were married. He asked those who were not if they were gay. A tiny minority admitted they were. When he wondered why men who said they were not gay sought out men instead of women ("lot lizards," such prostitutes are called), his fellow truckers claimed they had to pay females. The guys were free.

Most truck drivers, he learned, held a stereotypical view of gay men as effeminate. Gays were not real men, the thinking went—not, in other words, real men like truckers. Of course, when those same truckers felt an urge to get off, they had no problem letting another man go down on them.

Those conversations depressed Rod. The shame, fear, and even abhorrence surprised him. "Here I was getting to the point where I could admit being gay, and they did whatever they could to turn their back on it," he says. "It was ironic. Maybe they really weren't gay, but a lot of them sure liked having gay sex."

The more he looked, the more Rod found sex everywhere. He met men in the showers and bathrooms of highway rest areas, in nearby bushes, and in their own sleeper cabs. He learned that many hitchhikers near truck stops were young gay males. He listened, intrigued, to cryptic discussions on CB about those same cute hitchhikers.

On long drives, Rod thought about the personalities and attributes of the men with whom he shared the open road. Most were macho, individualistic, and independent. Many were not social creatures; being cooped up in a cab for hours a day, alone or with a sleeping partner, made them loners. They were mechanically inclined and did not mind working long, hard (if sometimes tedious) hours.

But long hours wear down even the most road-loving men, and after several years Rod felt the urge to settle down. He went back to Phoenix, attracted by the city's beauty, casual atmosphere, and natural splendor. Because he still loved driving, he got a job with a private-security armored truck company. The vast majority of his fellow drivers there are former military men on their second careers; the rest drive temporarily, waiting for police, fire, or civil service positions.

Armored-truck drivers differ from long-haul truckers—the risk factor when carrying around large amounts of money is far greater, and lifting and loading all that money is physically difficult—but the testosterone level is the same. Constant swearing, crude jokes, and a swaggering attitude help everyone get through the day.

However, Rod notes, at the security company attitudes toward gay men are a bit more relaxed. Perhaps, he says, that is because his current colleagues are more educated; the many men who have served in the military have been exposed to a number of different cultures and ways of life.

Yet it still took Rod a while to come out to coworkers. He wanted them to know him as a human being first. "After all, we carry side arms. If I don't know a guy well, there's no telling what he might do," he jokes. His coming-out process was casual. Once, for example, he responded to a fellow driver's comment about last night's date with a mention of his same-sex friend.

Today, Rod enjoys a nice level of intimacy with his colleagues. "On this job, you and the person you're working with are responsible for each other. Your life is in your partner's hands. You've got to have mutual respect. You're in the same truck eight or 10 hours a day. I talk about my life the same way I would if I was straight. Fortunately, I've never had anyone refuse to work with me. Maybe being open that way is my little contribution to educating the world about gay people. Today, everyone at my job knows we're just as normal, hard-working, courageous, and boring as straight people."

Outside of work Rod educates too. "Most of my gay friends tease me about driving an armored vehicle," he laughs. "They go, 'O-o-oh, you wear a gun and you drive a truck. You're so butch!' I take my uniform off as soon as I get home, but I think deep down my friends admire me because I've worked for so long in jobs that are traditionally straight. I guess it comes down to the fact that I like what I do. I've come to the conclusion that I can't allow the things people say or do—other guys at work or my friends outside work—to keep me from doing whatever it is I enjoy."

Victor Emovi

The 28 drivers for Scara-Mix resemble their counterparts at every other cement company. Some decorate their trucks with logos of their favorite football teams; others inscribe mottoes like "Rock and Roll!" on the doors. Many put their wife's and children's names on the front.

Victor Emovi's cement truck is personalized too. He stuck a rainbow flag on his window, and until a recent breakup he drove everywhere with the name of another man on the visor.

In the 15 years he has worked for the Staten Island, N.Y., company, the worst thing that ever happened to openly gay Victor occurred when a coworker borrowed his truck and placed duct tape over the rainbow. He told Victor, without rancor, that he had no problem with homosexuality; he just did not want anyone to think *he* was gay too.

"My name's still on the side of the truck," Victor retorted. "I don't think there would be a lot of confusion."

Being out as a cement truck driver has never been an issue for the 42-year-old New Yorker. And because he has always been up front and proud about his life, fellow drivers, bosses, and the customers he delivers concrete to all over Staten Island seldom bat an eye.

On the contrary, Victor's social and love lives are treated just like anyone else's. His former lover occasionally rode in the truck; if he called wondering what time dinner would be, the conversation went out over the two-way radio like any other couple's. When an unfamiliar face appears at a work site to say hi, everyone asks Victor if he has a new boyfriend—and hopes the answer is yes.

"We're in the 21st century now" is Victor's explanation of why a gay cement truck driver is a nonissue. "This is a family company, and everyone is like a family. I'm average height, a typical guy, and most people would never know I'm gay. But when they find out, even the big butch muscle guys seem to have no problem. Remember, this is New York. It's not like there's no gay people around. Everyone nowadays knows somebody who's gay."

Things were not always that easy. In high school Victor hid his homosexuality by dating girls. After graduation he joined the Air Force, and his coming-out process began. Yet he was not completely out until he was 26, when he met the man with whom he would spend the next 12 years. His mother and sister already suspected he was gay and accepted his confirmation calmly. His father, however, was quite distressed. For five years he and Victor did not speak.

When Victor joined Scara-Mix, he did not announce he was gay, but neither did he hide it. He hoped his coworkers would get to know him first as a good, hard-working man (and excellent bowler). Then, if anyone asked, he would tell the truth.

One day another driver came to Victor's house. He met Victor's lover, saw their bedroom, and said, "Don't take this the wrong way, man, but what's the deal?" Victor explained the deal, the coworker told others, and no one cared. As his colleagues became friends with Victor's boyfriend, "no big deal" turned into "genuine acceptance." The couple was invited to every company Christmas party and wedding. One morning Victor emblazoned his boyfriend's name on his truck. The congratulations poured in.

Other drivers feel comfortable telling Victor about their own relatives who are gay. (Because Staten Island is so small, he already knew most of them.) His colleagues as well share the latest gay jokes with Victor; they know he enjoys a good laugh. They show pictures of scantily clad women and ask good-naturedly, "Come on, don't you want that?" "Nah," he replies. "Been there, done that."

His rainbow flag does draw occasional stares, Victor admits, but he does not have to respond. Someone at the work site always says something first: "Yeah, he's been delivering concrete to us for 15 years. He's a good guy. No sweat."

Victor returns the easy acceptance. For years he and his lover threw an end-of-summer bash for 200 people. Cement truck drivers mingled with family and gay friends, and everyone got along great. To this day the word at work is that gay men throw the best parties and have the most fun.

Victor enjoys both the solitude of his truck and the easy relationships he has formed with fellow workers and customers. He drives five days a week in January and February, six days the rest of the year. With seniority (he's number 10 on the list) he has time to travel to Aruba each August, go hunting in November, and take off to places like Amsterdam when the opportunity arises. He never knows where he'll deliver to until he reports to work each morning, however, and that keeps life interesting. Because he has spent almost his entire life on Staten Island, he knows nearly every builder and contractor. He dresses in dungarees, a shirt, and baseball hat; he's never stressed out, and, thanks to the Teamsters union, when he retires at age 51 after 25 years of service he will collect a good pension and big annuity.

Victor has never had a major problem with the Teamsters. The one negative experience occurred when he tried to add his lover to the health plan. Victor explained that they owned a house together and shared a life but was told he needed a marriage certificate. Victor decided not to pursue the issue because his boyfriend already had good benefits through his phone company job. He believes that if he had followed up, he might have been able to affect change, but he feels the union will come around soon anyway.

He realizes that other cement truck drivers may not enjoy the 21st-century work environment he does. Another Staten Island company employed a transvestite, who recently began wearing skirts and pumps; several customers do not want him delivering to their sites, so to avoid losing accounts his bosses switched him to a dump truck. The man is considering a lawsuit for sexual harassment.

Victor has no such worries. In fact, right now his biggest gay-related issue concerns his truck. Drivers get a new one every four or five years, and Victor is about due. He is trying to decide if he should put a larger rainbow flag on the door—and, if so, whether to stick with a decal or actually paint it on.

VINCE CAWLEY: ELECTRICIAN

Vince Cawley remembers the day a new man arrived at the construction site. In the midst of running electrical wire, Vince asked if he wanted to have lunch. The newcomer said no, so Vince found someone else to head to Wendy's with. As usual, they brought food back, sat, and ate on the back of a truck.

Later that afternoon a coworker told Vince, "There's a lot of shit going on." The new worker had told his boss that Vince had come on to him, and rumors were flying around the job.

Vince felt a rush of emotions: anger, sadness, frustration, confusion. For the rest of the day he made himself scarce. Work went slowly, and at 10 P.M. most of the electrical crew was still there. Feeling he had to stand up for himself, Vince confronted the new worker's boss. "He should have talked to me," Vince said.

"You scared the kid," the boss countered.

Then Vince headed over to his own boss, a man he'd never had any reason to come out to. But Vince wanted to make sure his reputation stayed clean.

"I don't care about any of that shit," his boss said. "You're a good electrician. That's all that counts." And that was the end of that.

In 10 years as an electrician, working on projects large and small throughout Boulder, Colo., and Denver, that is the worst experience Vince has had. He has come out to hundreds of coworkers and bosses as well as a few homeowners. Invariably, he learns about their gay and lesbian relatives and friends. He has discussed his love life at work, then fielded suggestions on how to improve it. For 10 years he has enjoyed the respect and admiration of the men (and, on rare occasions, women) with whom he remodels homes and builds office towers, schools, and hospitals. They like him as a human being. The fact that he is gay means far less than his ability to run wire.

Electricians—all members of the construction industry, really—get a bum rap, Vince says. It is a male-oriented trade, and many of his coworkers do not read or write particularly well. But they are wonderful human beings with plenty of native intelligence and an extraordinary ability to create long-lasting structures using only blueprints, raw materials, their hands, and lore handed down from one generation of construction workers to the next.

"I have such huge respect for the guys I work with," Vince says. "These are not dumb guys from shop class or riffraff. They work so hard, they do so well, and at the same time they express such love for things: the world they live in, their kids. Sometimes it just blows me away."

Vince loves the life of an electrician, and he especially loves it in the Rocky Mountain town of Boulder. Construction work starts early, so most days begin with spectacular sunrises in the east. Job sites are often in the middle of nowhere—the whole point of his job, after all, is to create something out of nothing—so he has time to admire such sights as soaring hawks swooping down on prairie dogs.

He enjoys the ruggedness of his work: everything from the winds of winter and heat of summer to the fact that he is allowed to answer nature's call outside. The work is not heavy or laborious, but when the day is done he feels physically satisfied, like an athlete after a game. He likes measuring, making sure things fit well, and the satisfaction that comes from crafting work that will serve many people for many years. He appreciates the chance to chat with other workers before the day begins and when it ends. After all, the satisfaction of a job well done means little unless you can share it with others.

Though he seems like a natural-born electrician, Vince came relatively late to the trade. He was born and raised in Hamilton, N.Y., a small town best known as the home of Colgate University. Though there were only 500 students in his high school, that was crowded compared to his Catholic school eighth-grade class of 15. Vince's parents—his father was a car dealer, his mother a housewife—did their best to populate Hamilton: He has nine siblings, all older than he.

A vague feeling of differentness always lurked in the back of Vince's head, but for years he pushed it aside. Yet one night during senior year of high school he dreamed he was having sex with his best friend. Vince woke up almost paralyzed with fear. That day his world began to crumble.

Vince told his friend about the dream—not to make it happen but to ask for advice. Although the friend said the news did not bother him, he told his ex-girlfriend, who soon told Vince's ex-girlfriend. The rest of the year was difficult.

Despite his realization that he might be gay, it took another two years before he truly "got it," Vince says. That happened at the University of Rochester, a college he "fell into" because he was not sure what he wanted to do. In retrospect he would have preferred to go to a more liberal place like Oberlin, Antioch, or Deep Springs, but he stayed at Rochester, majored in art history, and graduated magna cum laude.

His favorite activity in college was working backstage at the Eastman School of Music, designing lighting and creating scenery. Vince enjoyed that physical work; he liked the feeling of arranging various elements in a certain way so they came together onstage in a tangible, aesthetically pleasing way. Working backstage on shows is remarkably similar to doing construction, he says: "You start with a goal, you work with your hands to achieve it, and in the end it either works or it doesn't." He never wanted to be onstage, but was delighted to see his work represented there.

After college Vince still did not know what he wanted to do. He spent time interning with a regional theater, then moved back in with his parents. That was no place for a college graduate, so on a whim he asked a friend if he wanted to move to Colorado. Vince had visited Boulder before, and it seemed to him like a place where "crazy kids who don't know what to do with their lives" could find themselves. The friend agreed, and Vince has been a Coloradan ever since.

He arrived in Boulder with no job prospects. But he had always called himself an electrician, so he opened the yellow pages and began calling contractors. One of the first men who answered asked if he was a journeyman or an apprentice. "I don't know," Vince replied. "Then you're an apprentice," the contractor told him.

Five days after pulling into Boulder, Vince was working as an apprentice electrician. The first tool he was handed was a hacksaw. As real electricians called out lengths, he cut wire for them. He was skinny, and the work was hard, but he persevered.

Coming out on the job was never an issue for Vince. He is proud of who he is as both a gay man and an electrician, and he recognizes—as do most others—that his sexuality has nothing to do with how well he wires buildings.

He comes out in various ways. Sometimes it is premeditated because he wants to share his life with another crew member. Sometimes it is spur-of-the-moment, when other people talk about their dates or he hears a comment he feels demands a response. Sometimes people are surprised. More often, they already suspected. Almost always, however, they tell him they feel honored he was able to tell them—and then they mention a relative, friend, neighbor, or former boss who is also gay. One man told stories about a cousin who attended family functions in drag; a "big huge bubba" announced that his stepbrother was gay. Two weeks later Vince and the bubba went snowboarding together.

Coming out to his colleagues opens many doors. The more Vince shares of his life, the closer his coworkers feel. One man felt comfortable enough, after hearing Vince talk about the man he was dating, to say, "I'm sorry, but I don't think this guy's good enough for you." Vince laughs as he recalls the advice. "It turned out he was right," he says. "I'd revealed enough about both him and me for this guy to realize my boyfriend was a horrible person. A lot of people probably don't think construction workers would have those insights or could say those things, but he came right out and said it, and I felt good he did."

Preconceptions work both ways, of course. Because he is college educated and articulate, many gay men don't believe Vince works in construction. He explains patiently that, yes, he really does wear a tool belt. One man once asked, "Aren't all construction workers pretty provincial?"

"Aren't all gay guys weak and effeminate?" Vince countered.

While he is out at most big jobs, Vince sometimes "passes" when doing side work for individual homeowners. That is because he would rather work than chat with most owners. Besides, he figures, he has been hired for his electrical talents, not as a sexuality educator. Once, however, as he wrote down directions to a house, he felt like saying, "Yeah, I know where that is. I used to bang a guy right down the road." As he arrived he was stunned to see that the owners were two women whose cars were plastered with inverted triangles. Vince said, "I'll give you the 'family' discount." But he never spoke the G word and, to this day, does not know if they knew what he was talking about.

Vince can count on the fingers of one hand the negative reactions he's gotten. There was the new crew member, mentioned earlier, who freaked out at a lunch invitation. Earlier, just two months into his career, Vince sat in silence as a coworker said it would be great if all gay people were herded into Denver's Mile High Stadium and attacked by lions. "I felt totally defenseless," Vince recalls with a mixture of anger and sorrow. "I was the new idiot who handed wire to everyone else. I didn't think I could say anything. Today, I'd go toe-to-toe about that crap, but back then I couldn't. Or at least I didn't think I could."

There was also the time another man, perched atop a ladder, launched into an antigay tirade. Before Vince could react, an apprentice walked over and shouted, "Shut up! I have gay friends, you know."

Later Vince thanked the apprentice. The young man stared at him and said, "I didn't do it for you. I really do have a lot of gay friends." That comment, Vince says, was humorous but also humbling. He realized that, although to his knowledge he is the only openly gay male construction worker in Boulder, his coworkers' worlds stretch far beyond than their job sites.

LARRY SMOOT:
UNION STAFF WORKER

Since early last century, labor unions have fought to improve the quality of life for American workers. They focus on tangible issues such as safety in the workplace and health benefits for families, as well as intangible ones like respect for the worker. Interestingly, those same issues mobilize many gay and lesbian activists. Yet for years unions and gay organizations waged their battles separately.

Few people in either the labor or gay movement recognized the connections between the two. When unions first gained strength, members were stereotyped as radicals marching outside mainstream America. Their demands were seen as outrageous attempts to upset the established social order. If they succeeded, the status quo warned, there was no telling how far our society would fall.

The status quo was wrong. Labor unions did succeed, and the country survived. In just a few generations union members moved from the fringes of American life to the middle of Middle America. Union members turned into the same people their predecessors had battled so fiercely. Then when a new group of outsiders—gays—demanded their place at the table, union members resisted. Granting legal rights and benefits to gay people, they proclaimed, would spell the beginning of the end of American society.

Recently, however, unions and gays have edged closer together. Gays are increasingly visible in union workplaces—not only at telecommunications companies and schools but on factory floors and in mines. They are demanding the same rights on the job—and from their union—as their straight coworkers and fellow union members. Union leaders, meanwhile, have discovered that reaching out to gay members and embracing their issues strengthens their union.

Larry Smoot, a 39-year-old Army veteran, has spent nearly a decade working in Washington, D.C., at the national headquarters of the Newspaper Guild. For six decades that union was the representative of media workers; in 1995 it merged with the Communications Workers of America. Yet for many years before his current job Larry believed unions to be "testosterone-filled, crime-ridden places." From childhood, when Larry heard the word "union," he imagined macho men with closed minds.

But now, Larry realizes the face of labor is changing. The people who oppose gay rights also support union busting. At the same time, rank-and-file members and their leaders who know openly gay men like Larry understand that issues like domestic-partner benefits have little to do with homosexuality and everything to do with working conditions and quality of life. The more unions recognize that gay people care as much as straights about decent contracts and taking care of their families—and that gay folks do have families, including children—the stronger both the labor and gay movements will be.

That revelation came slowly to Larry, a Wisconsin native. He knew as a young boy that he was gay, but he also knew that in the tiny town of Suring it was not something to talk about. He dated girls until he was 16, then stopped because they started to discuss marriage. He graduated from high school with no idea of what would come next. Like many young men in similar situations, he joined the Army. By his second day of basic training at New Jersey's Fort Dix, he realized homosexuality was incompatible with military service. His response, he says, was to "put my gayness in a separate room and lock it up."

He could stash his homosexuality away, but he could never forget it. Throughout basic training he was terrified someone would discover his secret and that the Army would dishonorably discharge him. Nevertheless, he committed himself to the Army, and he was determined to finish his tour.

Among the most difficult times was leave. Groups of soldiers partied in hotel rooms, and sexual escapades were common. One night his friends hired a prostitute. Everyone was expected to chip in for her fee and share in the fun. Larry offered his excuse in Army talk: "I'm not getting some fuckin' disease and watch my fuckin' dick fall off."

The ruse worked; no one suspected he was gay. When his tour was up and he returned to Wisconsin, he remained closeted. He continued to keep his secret during his five-year stint in the Army reserves and during his day jobs at local factories. "In that part of the state there was no way I could let anyone know," he says. "There was just no way at all to say it."

In 1985 he moved to Milwaukee and was hired as a security guard. But he found the work mind-numbing and, with as little foresight as the first time around, rejoined the Army. "I'd been hiding my homosexuality so long, I wasn't really good at thinking things through," he explains.

He became an administrative specialist (clerk-typist) at Fort Jackson, S.C. One day a 40-man airborne platoon came to the base for training. Six or eight members were clearly gay and did not care if anyone knew. Larry was flabbergasted. He wanted to learn more about these men but worried about what people would say if he was seen hanging out with them. He overcame his fears, and they took him to gay bars in nearby Columbia. The visits were frightening—

Larry was proud of his unblemished military record and wanted to keep it—but he could not stay away.

He was transferred to Fort Campbell, Ky., and assigned to a Special Forces aviation unit specializing in nighttime hostage rescues. It was such a macho environment, he says, that "you couldn't fit any more testosterone in. There were lots of airborne people—pretty nasty guys who burped, farted, and had total disregard for everything. Those were exactly the kind of people you needed for the job."

He spent four years at Fort Campbell, earning promotions and commendations. Unlike most of the men in his unit, he never boasted about sexual exploits with women. In fact, he rarely socialized with females. Some people figured out he was gay, and for the first time Larry did not care. He is certain his first sergeant knew but never asked. The man was more concerned with how Larry did his job, and Larry respected him for that.

Larry moved into off-post housing with another gay man. They were friends, not lovers, but rumors about the other man's homosexuality followed from his previous posting in Europe, and discharge proceedings were initiated. For the first time Larry questioned the military and his position in it. "I really believed in the uniform I wore," he says. "I truly felt I was protecting the Constitution and the freedoms we enjoy. I saw this witch-hunt as a direct conflict with that." Boldly, he spoke to his superiors about military hypocrisy.

A new first sergeant arrived: "The biggest country redneck I ever saw." The sergeant strongly advised Larry to move out of his house with the gay man. When he did not, the sergeant called him in and ordered him to move back into post barracks. Larry rolled his eyes. The man roared, "That's insubordination. If you do anything like that again, I will bring you up on charges."

The intimidation worked. Though gay bars in Nashville, an hour away, were not off-limits, Larry no longer went. He stopped hanging out with gay people. Still, the first sergeant burst into Larry's room at 2 A.M., drunk, announcing an "inspection" but hoping to catch Larry with another man. "I can't believe he thought I was that stupid," Larry says.

When an early-out program was announced, Larry reassessed his options. He wanted to stay in the Army but only if he could work in security. Getting such an assignment would have entailed a thorough background check, including discussions with friends and family in his hometown. By that time certain people knew he was gay, so Larry decided to leave the military. From the time his new first sergeant took over, he had not dated anyone or associated with gay people. He was so used to hiding his true self, it had become second nature.

Back home in Wisconsin, he got a job as manager of a group home for developmentally disabled people. And he lived with a man who made no attempt to hide his homosexuality. Larry's father—who, when Larry was 17, had asked "Are you one of those guys who likes guys better than girls?" and received a resounding "No!" in reply—asked again. This time Larry told the truth. His father said he still loved him—a response Larry was not sure he would hear. Tremendously relieved, Larry finally knew that leaving the service had been the right move.

In 1992 Larry needed a change. He moved to Washington, D.C., and was hired as mail clerk at the national headquarters of the Newspaper Guild. He had had little contact with unions and still thought they were run by "mob-run goons who would rather shoot gay people than talk to them." In addition, because then-president Chuck Dale seemed like someone from "the old school," Larry began work as a closeted man.

Gradually, however, he realized the union atmosphere was better than he thought. The national office was small, and although he was only a clerk, Larry's responsibilities for shipping, copying, and dealing with vendors made him indispensable. Chuck Dale, he came to see, may not have been comfortable with social change, but he was a man who worked hard to accept it. He was also, Larry says, "a straight-forward guy. The last thing he wanted was someone who tried to bull-shit him." Being in the closet was the ultimate bullshit.

Larry eased out of the closet at work. Away from the office life was also good: He found a lover. But two years later the man learned he had AIDS—and only nine T-cells. Within days he collapsed. Six months later he was dead.

Despite the trauma, that was in some ways a positive time for Larry. Throughout his personal hell the Newspaper Guild supported him. Colleagues treated him exactly like he was a straight man whose female partner was dying. They urged him to leave work, spend as much time at the hospital as he needed, and return when he could. The organization's national convention loomed, and Larry's expertise was vital. But everyone at the office pitched in and took up the slack.

"I had no energy to hide anything," Larry says. "I was totally vulnerable and open. They saw everything, and they responded so well. I commend everyone for that."

Of course, no workplace is perfect. The day his lover died, the office manager called Larry with a question about the postage meter. "He was dead in my house, and she asked me about that!" Larry says. "I had a lot of resentment for a long time."

Returning to the office, Larry threw himself into his work. He was promoted, and in 1995, when the 33,000-member Newspaper Guild merged with the 600,000-member Communications Workers of America, he unexpectedly moved into the ranks of gay union activists. A group of gay employees at the new organization began meeting to discuss workplace issues. They called themselves Lavender Lunch. Soon they joined Pride at Work, a national organization of gay, lesbian, bisexual, and transgendered workers and supporters founded the previous year to promote cooperation between the gay and labor communities. Activities include meetings, educational forums, marching in gay pride parades, even picketing in support of job actions. "People really notice our eye-catching, red-and-white GAY, LESBIAN, BISEXUAL, AND TRANSGENDER LABOR signs," Larry says, laughing.

Members come from a variety of unions, including Teamsters and other AFL-CIO trade groups. Pride at Work now boasts over 1,200 members in more than two dozen chapters across the nation. Each chapter tries to involve as many different unions as possible, and includes rank-and-file members as well as union staff workers.

Larry is treasurer for the Washington, D.C., chapter. He recently spoke about the group at the George Meany Center for Labor Studies and, to his surprise, found even people from the "macho building trades" to be open and accepting. Like other union members, he says, they realize that at the dawn of the 21st century, issues important to labor—wages, health benefits, pensions, workplace safety, and company-wide respect—are no different from gay issues.

"I know eyebrows get raised at first," Larry Smoot says proudly. "But it doesn't take long before straight people realize we're supporting the same causes and rights. They see we're working stiffs just like everyone else."

Ray Warren and Michael R. Sonberg: Judges

Ray Warren

Ray Warren is no different from any other North Carolinian who happens to be gay. Under state law he can be arrested, tried as a felon, and imprisoned for having sex with a same-sex partner.

Ray Warren is also unique: He is a Superior Court judge, sworn to uphold the law. In a stunning example of the disparity between 19th-century legislation and 21st-century reality, "Judge Ray"— that's the nickname by which everyone, including visitors to his Web site (www.judgeray.com), knows him—sits unimperiled on the bench. He banters as easily as ever with straight, conservative prosecutors and defense attorneys who respect his fairness and integrity.

The irony of his position is not lost on Judge Ray. In his soft, easy twang he notes that his hometown, Charlotte, is nicknamed "Queen City of the South." "I'm just doing my job," he chuckles.

"The universe of Southern white gay Republican Episcopal elected officials is kind of small," he adds. "Although, come to think of it, George W. Bush misses out by just one minor factor."

In his Superior Court post, Judge Ray administers his state's upper-level trial court. He has jurisdiction over felony criminal causes, civil cases involving amounts over $10,000, and appeals. He has adjudicated everything from medical malpractice suits to zoning disputes. He could, in theory, hear a sodomy ("crimes against nature") felony case. However, in his first six years on the bench he did not try one gay-related case.

Yet if he was assigned one, Judge Ray would not disqualify himself. "Why should I?" he asks. "A gay person has no more reason to do that than a black judge would in a civil rights case or a woman judge in a sex discrimination suit. We all bring things to the table because of who we are and where we come from, and we all have to set those things aside as a judge. If you can't do that, you shouldn't be sitting on the bench."

If it sounds as if Judge Ray has a strong sense of self, it's because he does. It is clear by his actions as well as his words that he wears his identity as a gay man as easily as his judicial robes. It is surprising, then, to learn that Judge Ray did not come out to another human being until 1998, when he was 40 years old. Even more astonishing, he had come out to himself only one year earlier.

For a man who comprises half the total number of openly gay elected officials in North Carolina—the other is the mayor of a small, liberal college town—Judge Ray lived a remarkably unremarkable first 38 years. He describes his grandparents as "typical Southerners: fervently patriotic conservatives who hated the federal government and also took advantage of VA, FHA, and college loans, and Social Security." As an enlisted man in the Army, his father learned of a world beyond Mooresville, N.C., where "Republicans, blacks, Catholics, Jews, and other exotic beings proved to be as normal as himself."

Judge Ray grew up bookish and introverted in and around Charlotte, but he was also an avid Eagle Scout who attended leadership school in New Jersey. In 1975 he enrolled in the University of North Carolina at Wilmington. Before graduating cum laude as a history major he acted in plays, served as a student senator, was elected chief justice of the student supreme court, and joined the cheerleading squad and Alpha Phi Omega service fraternity. A fervent Reaganite, Ray founded the UNCW College Republican Club.

He also dated women. In 1979, the same year he graduated, Ray got married. In fall 1980 he entered the University of North Carolina School of Law. There, he continued his conservative activism, publishing an alternative to the liberal college newspaper and moving beyond Chapel Hill to become chairman of the state Republican Party platform committee. He received his degree in 1983 and returned to Charlotte to practice law.

In 1984, just 27 years old, he was elected to the state House of Representatives. Reelected two years later, he served as deputy minority leader for 35 Republicans. He divorced, remarried, lost a race for North Carolina Secretary of State, returned to private practice, and in 1990 was appointed by Gov. Jim Martin to fill a vacancy on the Superior Court. He served as a delegate to the 1992 Republican national convention, where he helped nominate George Bush for president (after voting for Pat Buchanan in the primary). In 1994 he was elected to a full eight-year superior court term.

Today, he describes his 1997 self as "a little Dan Quayle, with more common sense but without the family money." He was a respected judge with a beautiful wife, two wonderful children, a nice home, and financial security.

Almost overnight his world turned upside down.

As part of his job, Judge Ray traveled around the state to hear cases. One night in the mountains, bored and away from his family, he logged on to America Online. He had heard about chat rooms but never visited any. That evening he did. The first gay-themed rooms he wandered into seemed stupid. He was so naïve that he used his main screen name, and so ignorant that his first Instant Message stunned him. "How the hell did you do that?" he typed back. It was his introduction to immediate conversation with a total Internet stranger.

But he did not communicate any further that night. Rattled, petrified, and feeling exposed, knowing that someone could enter his computer so easily, Judge Ray logged off. He vowed to stay off forever.

Less than 24 hours later, though, he was back on.

To this day, Judge Ray's mother claims the Internet made him gay. At the time, he himself could not have explained what impelled him—a seemingly straight man with an all-American family and a prestigious job—to seek out a gay chat room. But with a bit of perspective, he recognizes his entire life to that point was not what it seemed. "I'm starting to realize now that at some level I always knew," he says. "Coming of age in the South, I thought that being gay was the same as slaughtering babies and drinking their blood. I had no concept you could be both masculine and gay. Now I do remember thinking about it in seventh grade but not understanding it because I wasn't effeminate. I'm remembering a lot more now."

He believes his introversion was a direct result of his unrecognized struggle to hide his homosexual urges. For someone once so unknowledgeable about AOL, he used a sophisticated technological analogy to explain: "It takes so much computing power to run a virtual copy of yourself over the operating system that's already there. The computer that is my brain created an interface for the world that was acceptable to the world in which I lived. The virtual Ray Warren really was straight. He wasn't real, but he was all anyone saw. The real me ran in the background, in hidden files that even I did not see. Many of those times I thought I was shy, I was just out of RAM. I needed to shut down, clear files, and reformat the system."

Soon Judge Ray met a man and had his first same-sex encounter. He spent a year struggling with his feelings (and learning that chatroom participants "can't accurately measure their own anatomy, calculate their age, or use a bathroom scale"). It was an intense and difficult period, but he knows he is lucky; plenty of gay people spend decades feeling that way. He knows too that his timing was not random:

Around 40, many men who have denied their true selves suddenly lose the ability to maintain their "virtual lives."

It did not take Judge Ray long to realize this was not a midlife crisis but rather a chance to become the human being nature intended him to be. In spring 1998 he received another Instant Message asking starkly: "Are you gay, bi, or what?" Up to that point he had always answered, "I don't believe in categories." But the virtual Ray program was crashing, and in response he typed "Gay." He stared at the word in amazement, then hit SEND.

On July 22 of that year he repeated that word to his wife. She was "a loving, passionate woman, my best friend, the mother of my children," and he had no intention of leaving her. At the same time he knew he could not continue his life without revealing the news. He told her he was willing to forgo any physical relationship with a man, but said he had to have gay friends and a gay "life." She said she needed more than that from a husband.

The next six weeks were horrendous. The couple went to counseling, but their marriage could not last. On September 1, Judge Ray moved out.

But of all Judge Ray's memorable dates, none is more momentous than December 9, 1998. That morning, in the midst of President Clinton's impeachment crisis—when it was clear the rules of American society had changed and political leaders no longer had private lives—the superior court judge walked into packed press conferences in North Carolina's two major cities and outed himself.

In a month he was scheduled to rotate courts. He would be 200 miles away, deep in the mountains. He did not want his time there to be interrupted by a surprise phone call from a reporter, nor did he care to worry if anyone was watching where he went or who came into his home. If his homosexuality was a loaded gun, as he perceived it to be, Judge Ray wanted to be the one pulling the trigger.

He thought his first announcement, in Raleigh, went well. In addition to the news media, the room held a few friends and supporters. Driving to the second event, three hours away in Charlotte, he and the man he was dating speculated about the reaction there.

They knew that earlier in the morning, in advance of his press conferences, *The Charlotte Observer* had broken his story.

The room there was filled to overflowing. This time the press was outnumbered by men and women the judge worked with: prosecutors, district attorneys, deputy sheriffs, probation officers. As he walked in, they rose in a thunderous ovation. "They knew me as a human being before they knew me as a gay person," he explains. "They appreciated my work as a judge, and that was what really counted."

For a couple of days Judge Ray's homosexuality was front-page news in North Carolina. One of the most critical remarks came from the executive director of the state Republican Party, who said, "We trusted him. He has betrayed that trust. What a sad situation. Ray Warren has misled the people he represents, and he has destroyed his family with his deviant and destructive behavior."

Quickly, however, it became a nonissue. Of more than 500 E-mails, cards, and letters, only an insignificant few were negative. The positive response, meanwhile, was heartwarming. Deputy sheriffs, a tough breed who provide courtroom security, told Judge Ray his revelation had changed their view of gay people. Conservative Republicans were fully supportive. That reaction proves, the judge says, that being out on one's own terms is the most effective weapon gays have. Once someone knows a gay person, he can never again divide the world into "us" versus "them."

He knows, of course, that not everyone is pleased to have a gay judge. State law prohibits any nonvaginal intercourse with anyone who is not a spouse. A county commissioner tried to get Judge Ray removed for that reason. The effort failed, and the judge thinks he knows why. "Because there is no statute of limitations, most judges in North Carolina are probably felons too," he says, relishing the irony. "The number who have had oral sex or sex outside of marriage is probably phenomenal. If they went after me, they'd have to go after all of them, and I just can't imagine something like that happening."

So not only is Judge Ray not worried about being prosecuted for sodomy, he has begun actively speaking out on gay issues. He writes letters to the editor. He lectures on college campuses, and to civic and church groups. On his Web site he posts articles about such topics as religion, relationships, and gay Republicans. Although he cannot discuss pending cases, he also cannot remain silent about the importance of integrating gays into the fabric of American society.

"Being a judge does hamper me. Speaking out is not a conflict of interest, but I do go up to the line of what's permissible," he admits. "But minority judges have a long history of activism. Thurgood Marshall did not quit being a civil rights figure when he was named to the Supreme Court."

Invoking the name of another trailblazing African-American, he asks, "Why did Rosa Parks not give up her bus seat? The problem is not with speaking out; it's with not speaking out. It's funny—I've wanted to make a difference all my life, but this type of involvement was certainly not on my radar screen. I entered politics as a Goldwater Republican—'get rid of government!'—and now I'm talking about the need for government to protect me and acknowledge me as a full, legal human being. We say this is a land of opportunity, equality, and fairness for all. I want to make sure that includes people like me."

There are those who wish he were quieter. An attorney warned him that he risks losing the next election. He replies, "It's easy for straight people to think minorities should be quiet. But unless you're a minority, you don't understand."

His advocacy may yet cause problems. Judge Ray is up for re-election in 2002. Although he would like to prove that an openly gay person can be elected to public office in North Carolina, he feels he might effect more change off the bench, where he would be free to address any topic. Then he thinks about his two young children, years away from college, and realizes he can't give up his "day job."

Nowadays, Judge Ray's life is full, and it does not revolve solely around the judiciary. He hikes, cycles, Rollerblades, and plays volleyball. He loves Motown, country, and classical music. He reads Jane Austen and Dickens as well as books on physics, theology, and meteorology. He and his partner are active members of St. Peter's

Episcopal Church in Charlotte. Their lives center around Judge Ray's children, yard work, home projects, and everyday errands.

Coming out has not changed much, except that the partner he does those activities with is a man. However, one aspect of his life has changed a great deal: Judge Ray is no longer a staunch Republican. "I want to use the ambitions and talents I have, and it is abundantly clear no Republican governor or president would give me any consideration," he states. "And I don't mean appointing me to a high-paying job. I'm talking about little committees. I've been in government since I was 27, but the party I've been affiliated with has no interest in me."

For 37 years Ray Warren considered himself a straight white Southern man. For the last three he has realized he is gay. With that understanding has come a deeper appreciation of all minorities. But one thing has not changed: He remains a chauvinistic Southerner, intensely proud of his region—foibles, flaws, and all. "I've lived here all my life," he says. "As a gay man it's difficult, but it's changing rapidly. My own case is a perfect example. I came out as a gay man, but I still sentence people, I go to lunch with my deputies, and nothing has changed. I still hold court in small rural counties. In fact, I just got back from six months in Gaston County. My entire time there I wore an earring. That might not seem like a big deal to you, but anyone who's been there knows that is an amazing step forward."

And the fact that no one said a word those entire six months might be the most remarkable story of all.

Michael R. Sonberg

The Bronx Criminal Court of the City of New York looks as intimidating as it sounds. The massive concrete courthouse occupies an entire block in the shadow of Yankee Stadium, one of the few attractions in New York's most forlorn borough. Manhattan, all glitter and glitz, lies just a river away. Brooklyn and Queens, home to upwardly mobile citizens from nearly every country on earth, are geographically close too, but demographically worlds away. Suburban Staten Island might as well be on another planet.

The Bronx is almost entirely black and brown—and poor. Few of the borough's citizens have shared in the recent economic boom that rejuvenated the rest of New York City. The signs are everywhere: Bronx streets are more decrepit, the sidewalks filthier, the buildings shabbier, the faces more lined and downtrodden.

Inside the courthouse a river of humanity throngs the linoleum hallways. They are African-American, Hispanic, young, old, able-bodied, wheelchair-bound, defiant, submissive. Some have enormous families; others are utterly alone. Some seem visibly gay: They are flamboyant, outrageous, exaggeratedly masculine or feminine.

The gay judge is none of the above.

Judge Michael R. Sonberg's ninth-floor chambers are like his sexuality: largely hidden from public view. His workplace is accessible via special elevator, and the furnishings—real carpeting, polished desk, comfortable leather chairs—contrast vividly with the battered chairs and scuffed floors elsewhere in the building.

So too does Judge Sonberg stand out from the mass of bodies coursing through the courthouse, itself strained to the breaking point—running two shifts, 16 hours a day, seven days a week. He is slim and fit, looking every inch the middle-aged runner he is. He sports suspenders, a neatly trimmed, graying goatee, and, in late winter, a healthy tan. As he gazes around his office—plush compared with his courtroom, threadbare when contrasted with the workplace of a New York lawyer in private practice—he smiles easily.

Judge Sonberg is doing what he loves. And he is doing it on his own terms.

It has been nearly 15 years since that day in the mid '80s when Michael—then a Manhattan corporate attorney specializing in commercial and matrimonial litigation—picked up the form that marks the first step to becoming a judge. New York City mayor Edward Koch had already appointed the state's first openly gay judge, but Michael found the length and detail of the 20-page application daunting, so he put it aside.

In March 1990, however, Mayor David Dinkins spoke at the annual dinner of the Bar Association for Human Rights, expressly describing his desire to name more lesbians and gay men to the bench. Inspired, Michael requested a new application and submitted it in July. His 10 references included an impressive mix of straight people and gays. He heard nothing for months. Then a year later he was summoned home from a Canadian Rockies vacation for an interview with Mayor Dinkins. Within two weeks he was sworn in as a judge. Mayor Dinkins reappointed him twice, and Mayor Rudolph Giuliani reappointed him as well. Michael was one of six openly gay judges appointed during Mayor Dinkins's four-year term; through Mayor Giuliani's first seven years Michael was one of only two.

Judge Sonberg is aware of his rare status. "Since I was appointed as a gay man, part of my job is to be open," he says. That, however, is not easy to do. Being a judge is a very straight job, he declares. He cannot wear lavender robes or an AIDS ribbon. So his openness must be expressed in other ways.

He cites one example: Earlier that week he accepted the plea bargain of a 35-year-old man who gave oral sex to young boys after luring them with Pokémon cards. A lawyer who did not know that Judge Sonberg is gay described the defendant's "deviance" as homosexuality.

"No," the judge replied sharply. "That deviance is pedophilia." Many colleagues would not have recognized the distinction; few would have felt compelled to comment on it from the bench for the court record.

Incidents like that are, he admits, relatively rare. The bulk of Judge Sonberg's work consists of routine arraignments. New York courts are the busiest in the world. On a typical day he disposes of or adjudicates 100 cases. They range from disorderly conduct to murder and include everything in between.

"Everything" occasionally means gay-related cases. An infinitesimal percentage of the 15,000 or so cases Judge Sonberg handles each year involves identifiably gay, lesbian, bisexual, or transgendered people. The largest number are transvestite prostitutes and male hustlers; his own sexual orientation, he says, is irrelevant in those cases. He knows that some portion of the drug addicts, drug sellers, drunk drivers, car thieves, and shoplifters he sees are gay, but in those cases too the judge's homosexuality matters not at all.

However, every once in a while Judge Sonberg feels the need to speak about homosexuality from the bench. It usually happens during same-sex domestic-violence cases. Addressing the batterer, he speaks directly from the heart. Judge Sonberg mentions Andy, his life partner for 20 years, and describes their relationship as one based on love and respect, not hitting and hurting. He tells the defendant that anger and violence have no place in any relationship.

Defendants often seem surprised—less at the message than at the man who delivers it. "I really think lawyers should tell their clients beforehand that the judge is gay," he says dryly.

Judge Sonberg knows that, oaths of impartiality aside, he (like any judge) is only human. "I may evaluate an arraignment case differently because it's same-sex," he admits. "I may be tougher than the prosecutor wants, because a lot of prosecutors are young and feel uncomfortable discussing issues of sexuality. Sometimes I even ask out loud, 'Is this a same-sex relationship?' There are times I can look at the defendant and pretty much tell, but other times I don't know if it's that or simply neighbor against neighbor."

Besides same-sex domestic-violence arraignments, Judge Sonberg says his sexuality could influence his actions during jury selection. To his knowledge, in the Bronx no potential juror has ever self-identified as gay. ("With people of color, homosexuality is not always well accepted," he explains.) However, because jurors' attitudes toward homosexuality might be relevant in particular cases—gay bashings, sexual assaults, or altercations after a bar pickup—his voir dire questions in those instances might be very directed. Judge Sonberg has not had any cases like those above, but he can easily imagine a scenario in which he would ask potential jurors if they had any family members, coworkers, neighbors, or close friends whom they knew to be gay. He would follow up to find out if and how they socialized. He would probably also ask about religious affiliations, to ascertain if their faith held any position on gay people and whether they agreed with it.

Those types of questions, he notes, are apt to elicit a more useful reply than a more general "Do you have any feelings about gay people?"

Judge Sonberg believes it important to raise his colleagues' consciousness in this area. When he leads judicial education workshops on the topic of jury selection, he reminds listeners to replace questions like "What is your marital status?" with "Are you in a committed relationship with someone?"

"I think jurors' attitudes toward gay people are important," he says firmly. "Not everyone on the bench agrees."

Judge Sonberg recognizes that his position carries tremendous power and responsibility. Being a judge is, he says, "as lonely a job as exists, short of president of the United States." Judicial decisions are not made collaboratively, and judges face tremendous restrictions on the First Amendment rights of free speech and association. Judge Sonberg will not enter any place that, though legal, could cause embarrassment—a strip club, for instance—and he is not allowed to speak out, even privately, on a wide range of issues, from cases pending anywhere in the country to news topics of the day that might conceivably land in court. Some jurisdictions expressly prohibit judges from marching in gay pride parades, deeming them political events. For the past decade, however, Judge Sonberg has marched with colleagues, spouses, family, and friends in the Manhattan parade. The reaction from the crowd has been quite positive—especially from people of color, he says. He and his fellow judges did not, however, march in the Stonewall 25 parade in 1994 because they felt there was a "clear political agenda" to that march.

The loneliness Judge Sonberg cites extends to life off the bench. Old friendships are fine, he says. But those based on the law alone are hard to maintain once one person joins the judiciary. Judges tell lawyer jokes and vice versa. "That's why a lot of my friends are judges—or, at least, not lawyers," he says. His partner's brother was elected to the Long Island bench in 1998, giving the Bronx judge something in common with at least one in-law.

"I've never gotten up in the morning and not wanted to come to work," Judge Sonberg says. "But there are lots of afternoons when I don't want to return the next day. It's not easy dealing with so much depressing stuff day after day. This is not a very happy place. There are a lot more stories of failure than success."

So why does he remain on the bench, especially one in the very depressing Bronx Criminal Court? "Somebody has to," he replies. "I know that sounds flip, but this is important work. It needs to be done by people who have the intellect to do it properly, who have a strong sense of personal justice. It's exciting making sure the rules embedded in our Constitution are followed. Who else gets to enforce the Bill of Rights in his job? And I love everything about the law: the research, the writing, the advocacy. This is the purest form of that I know."

Judge Sonberg's story is unique for a New Yorker growing up in the '60s and '70s: He did not come out until 1979, when he was 31. Even then, he still had not had sex with a man. He was terrified of losing his friends—many of them lawyers—but, carrying a camera for "cover," he finally attended Pride Day. He was stunned to see a man he knew: Hank Henry, who, like Michael, was active in court reform issues. But Michael had always seen Hank in a suit and tie; this time he wore a tight-fitting tank top and several items of leather.

A few weeks later Michael found the courage to call Hank and ask if they could meet to discuss personal issues. Hank, who already suspected that Michael was gay, agreed. They met after one of Michael's therapy sessions. "I don't remember anything my therapist said, but I do remember talking with Hank for hours that night," Judge Sonberg recalls. "He was warm, encouraging, informative, and non-judgmental—everything I had hoped for in my first out conversation with another gay man." After dinner Hank took him to his first gay bar—as well as his second, third, and fourth. (They had to sneak into the Ramrod because Michael was wearing a Lacoste shirt instead of the requisite leather).

"Hank seemed to know every bartender and half the patrons," Michael says in awe. The evening ended many hours later in front of Hank's apartment building with a very public show of affection from Hank. Judge Sonberg says he will never forget his first kiss—even if ever-gentlemanly Hank kept his lips closed. The judge also will never forget the man he calls his mentor. Hank died at age 49 in 1995, just 12 days before Judge Sonberg's swearing-in.

With Hank's help Michael joined a gay lawyers group. Twenty years later, many of the men he met through that organization remain his friends. He also started running, which improved his low self-esteem, and joined New York's gay synagogue, Congregation Beth Simchat Torah, which improved his social life. And in 1980 he met Andy.

Judge Sonberg now sees a strong connection between his identities as a gay man and a Jew; both groups are considered "outsiders" by some. While the judge's differences are not readily apparent, their very existence means there are people who hate him. That knowledge has focused his attention on the persecution of minorities and the rights of individuals. Though he has not experienced blatant discrimination himself, he does identify with society's outsiders. "That's a valuable perspective to bring to this job," he says. "I'm part of the Establishment and also a despised minority. I've learned to live with both roles."

Although Judge Sonberg has limited opportunities to be open in his courtroom, he finds ways to be out in other areas of work. Many police officers assigned to the courthouse—as well as corrections officers, security guards, bailiffs, clerks, and other support personnel—know Andy by name because the judge talks proudly of their life together. When Judge Sonberg appeared on the cover of *Newsweek*'s "Gay Today" issue in early 2000, he received heartfelt congratulations from many court workers. Still, he knows that homophobia lurks not far below the surface. Why else, he wonders, are there no openly gay court officers, only four defense attorneys, and—out of 400—fewer than a dozen assistant Bronx district attorneys?

The ranks of out gay judges is equally thin. Judge Sonberg ticks off the figures: Fourteen New York State court judges out of nearly 600 (and all of them are from New York City); one lesbian U.S. federal court judge; 110 on the entire International Association of Lesbian and Gay Judges mailing list. The reasons are often political—some judges must run for election; others are appointed by elected officials who see no advantage to naming openly gay judges—but the numbers still mark an improvement from 1979. That was the year Michael Sonberg came out—and also, in California, the year Gov. Jerry Brown appointed the first openly gay judge anywhere in America.

For over a decade now, Judge Sonberg has dispensed justice to a never-ending stream of humanity in the Bronx. His courtroom may be dilapidated, but it is not dull. In fact, just the day before this interview, as he finished sentencing a defendant, the man turned and yelled at the bench, "Cocksucker!"

The judge did not bat an eye. "He probably saw my picture in *Newsweek*," Judge Michael Sonberg told the court with a confident, completely out grin.

Larry Montero: Death Care Worker

Some little boys know exactly what they want to be when they grow up: a doctor or lawyer, perhaps, or maybe a firefighter or police officer. As far back as Larry Montero can remember, he dreamed of becoming a funeral director.

With a passion and intensity that some men reserve for describing their greatest sexual encounter or the most unforgettable ball game they ever saw, the 41-year-old Tampa native describes his earliest memories of what was then called "undertaking" and in the 21st century has been rechristened as "death care." "I always wanted to be in a profession people look up to and admire. Where I lived, that meant two things: priests and funeral directors," he says, his words spilling over each other in a soft Southern twang that has no doubt reassured thousands of grief-stricken customers. "My grandmother lived next door to a funeral home, and every year we'd go visit. Every time a body came in she would call me, and I'd watch. I'd stand in amazement as the body was laid out, embalmed, and put in the casket. A few days later I'd watch as it left with an escort. Most people didn't want anything to do with death, but the funeral director gave me a crate to stand on so I could have a better view." While his friends played doctor, Larry and the undertaker's daughter played "funeral." She played the organ, and he conducted the service using a cardboard box for a casket.

In fifth grade Larry's class held a Career Day. Other children looked ahead and saw themselves as professional athletes, business executives, politicians, and FBI agents. Larry drew a picture of "Montero Funeral Home," complete with graveyard. He has never forgotten that image. There is a good reason: The drawing now hangs in his office at Infinity Cremations, the Fort Lauderdale company he owns.

Larry's father was a Cuban immigrant from the pre-Castro days, who began working as a milk deliverer and worked his way up to vice president of the dairy company. Larry's mother, a housewife, hailed from southern Alabama. Whenever the family traveled, Larry would eagerly open the yellow pages, turning to "Funeral Homes." He examined all the listings and studied every logo. The funeral business was in his blood—and he could not wait to learn how to drain blood, replace it, and embalm a body.

Larry dreamed of attending one of the two best mortuary colleges in the United States—one was in Atlanta, the other in Cincinnati—but while he was in high school his father died at the age of 51. For financial reasons Larry ended up in Miami, at Florida's only in-state mortuary college.

Like most mortuary students, he had plenty of opportunities for hands-on work. Many funeral homes hire students as cheap labor. They answer phones at night and help move and embalm bodies. (Only recently, he says, has the Federal Trade Commission begun regulating the industry more closely.) Larry interned at a Hollywood, Fla., funeral home located in a beautiful old mansion. He lived there too.

Larry's father's death had enabled him to come out of the closet. Cuban men, he says, despise homosexuality, so he kept quiet when his father was alive. But moving from Tampa to Miami was as incredible a change as when the black-and-white *Wizard of Oz* switched to color. In the late '70s, Larry says, South Florida was "totally gay." He jumped headlong into the scene, which featured copious amounts of drugs and alcohol. His apartment above the magnificent funeral home was the scene of frequent wild parties. Though emotionally (and sometimes physically) draining, the life of a funeral worker is not grim.

After finishing the two-year college program, Larry was hired by a Fort Lauderdale funeral home. Around the same time he fell in love with Nicky, a Cuban man who had arrived on the Mariel boat lift and worked in another part of the death care industry: the medical examiner's office. Larry suddenly had everything he ever wanted: a job in a funeral home and a companion. But it did not last. Nicky was diagnosed as HIV-positive in April 1984. Two months later he was dead.

Even though at work he had been surrounded by death, to that point Larry had dealt with only one or two AIDS cases. He knew the precautions to be taken: The bodies were placed in double-zippered pouches and immediately cremated, without embalming or viewing. Fear of AIDS permeated the death care industry.

Larry and his lover's family wanted Nicky to be embalmed, cosmeticized, and viewed, but in the funeral home prep room the owner told Larry that neither he nor his son would do the embalming. "In fact," he told Larry, "with your lifestyle, you'll probably get AIDS sometime. So if you want to embalm him, you can."

Larry did not want to—not from fear of AIDS but because of worries he could not handle the emotional impact. It would have been, he says, like a doctor operating on a spouse or child. However, he adds, if he had to, he would have. Finally, though, someone in another funeral home agreed to embalm Nicky's body. There was a viewing after all, followed by burial in Fort Lauderdale. Larry says that to his knowledge this was the first time in the area that a person who had died of AIDS complications received a "full service" funeral.

For four years after Nicky's death Larry threw himself into two things: work and play. He does not know now whether he worked in order to party or partied in order to work, but he does know that as much as he loves the death care industry, it has a down side. Funeral directors routinely work more than 60 hours a week, and much of that time is spent doing difficult tasks: talking to people who have just lost a loved one, transporting bodies, arranging services. Even when they are not actually working, funeral directors are on call. "This is a 24-hour-a-day business," Larry says. "You can't tell someone whose husband or wife or parent or child has just died, 'We'll be there tomorrow.' "

In 1987 Larry was arrested and convicted of driving under the influence and lost his driver's license. In his industry that was virtually a death sentence: A worker who is unable to drive a funeral coach or limousine, pick up bodies and flowers, or make runs to the cemetery is worthless. Larry was fired. He appealed his dismissal to a state board, which ruled that, although he was terminated with just cause, he could collect unemployment benefits.

Shortly thereafter, Larry joined a recovery program. He found work with a car rental company at Miami International Airport and, thanks to his ability to sell upgrades and insurance, earned good commissions. But he longed to return to the profession he loved. With his driver's license back in hand, Larry was hired by a company that provided services to funeral homes. He worked in their office and also drove a funeral coach.

He was happy. However, at that time the death care industry was undergoing major changes. Family-owned funeral homes were being bought out by large conglomerates. (Currently, three companies dominate the funeral industry. Although many funeral homes retain family names, most are owned by enormous corporations.) He began to realize, he says, that he no longer worked in a profession. Death care had become a business.

Discouraged, Larry went to a job counselor. He took a battery of tests and found he was best suited to two types of jobs: forest ranger... and funeral director.

Reinvigorated, he moved to Key West and planned to open his own funeral home. He was welcomed by the gay and AIDS communities there, but the reception from the existing funeral homes was far different. He faced a number of regulatory roadblocks—put in place, he believes, with at least the tacit approval of the existing funeral homes—and returned to the Miami area.

Larry had been living with HIV since 1984. He learned he was positive the same week Nicky died. Through his volunteer work he knew that people with AIDS did not have much money to spend on dying. "I was seeing a lot of hairdressers, bartenders, and waiters—people who had not always claimed all their income, so when they went on disability they were not receiving a lot of Social Security," he explains. "Also, because people with AIDS are younger, they haven't prepared for death like older people do, by prepaying their burials or buying death insurance. And, of course, they don't have a lot of life insurance either."

When he began advising members of HIV/AIDS groups how to save money while dying, someone suggested he open a cremation business. At an average cost of $1,000, cremations cost far less than burials, which have ballooned to between $8,000 and $12,000. It was an excellent idea. Larry realized that once again he could provide a vital service, in a respectful way, in a line of work he loved. Just as important, he could help members of his own community.

So Larry went back to school and received certification to open a crematory. In January 1996 he founded Infinity Cremations. (A crematory picks up a body, holds it for 48 hours after receiving a death certificate, then cremates it and places the cremains in an urn.) He spread the word about Infinity through AIDS organizations and his Metropolitan Community Church. The first day of operation a good friend's lover died of AIDS, and Larry headed out on his first death call.

He had 36 calls that first year. Today, he answers over 200 annually. His primary focus, he says, is offering a low-cost alternative to burial to everyone in South Florida, especially the gay and AIDS communities. Each morning he goes to work joyfully. His job is not about death at all, he says; it is about helping survivors get through the worst moments of their lives.

Of course, he says, as a business owner he must spend time wondering how to bring customers through the door. But he prefers to focus on the helping aspect of his work. Many people are referred by AIDS agencies, recovery groups, and the medical examiner's office. Those who make referrals know he does a good job at a reasonable price and that he treats everyone with dignity and respect. In return, Larry is buoyed by the grateful cards and letters he receives. On World AIDS Day he won South Florida AIDS Network's Care Award, beating out the likes of American Express. When he was just an employee at funeral homes, he seldom heard thanks.

Larry is very out in the gay community and advertises in gay and lesbian publications. However, in times of stress, people are not always sure who they are dealing with. Once he made a house call to a lesbian whose mother had just died. After Larry explained the crematory procedures, the woman asked, "Are you gay? Because if you're not, you're the nicest straight man I've ever met."

He does not place a rainbow sticker on his door, he says, because some people might feel uncomfortable—and there is no reason for anyone in a service industry to drive away those in need of service. In the beginning he printed two sets of brochures. He sent one to customers who learned about him through the gay community; the other went to those who heard of him from other sources. One day he fielded a call from an elderly woman who said she and her husband liked what they saw, including the price. However, she had one question: What did he mean by "HIV-owned and -operated"? Larry realized he had sent them the "gay" brochure. He thought for a moment then replied, "It's sort of like an HMO." The woman said, "Oh, that's fine. Come by tomorrow and we'll sign the contract." These days Larry no longer feels the need for two different brochures.

Although he is openly gay, Larry notes that he is a rarity in the death care industry. Most gay workers are closeted, and those who are out usually have little contact with the public. He says that one funeral home in his county is owned by a gay man, yet virtually no one knows. He tells about a gay man who works as an employee in another funeral home, but because the man is out, he is "hidden" in the prep room. "A lot of our business is about public relations," Larry explains. "Funeral directors are members of Kiwanis, the Rotary, every organization you can think of. That's how they network and generate business. Working with AIDS and pride organizations, like gay people do, just isn't the same. And how many gay men do you know who socialize by playing golf? So the gay guys in this industry tend to stay in the closet and act like they're straight."

Which is not to say that gay people are rare in death care. "It's a service-type industry," Larry says. "And gay people tend to want to provide services to others. It's an 'event' business, just like catering or party planning. There's good money to be made here. And as for me, I've always enjoyed doing prep work, like cosmetics and hair—I guess that's my gay gene."

Still, openly gay crematory owners are rare. Rarer still are gay crematory owners who are openly HIV-positive. In 1998 Larry's openness earned him a profile in *Poz* magazine—which in turn led to several date and marriage proposals. More gratifying, he says, were the letters and E-mails from people in small towns around the country who told him they wished they had someone like Larry to help with their own dying process or that of a loved one.

Although he plans to open a branch of Infinity Cremations in Tampa, Larry has no plans to become a conglomerate—he knows that retaining the personal touch is vital. So although he cannot assist everyone in America who needs death care, he helps as many in his own special gay and AIDS communities as he can. That is Larry Montero's childhood dream. And—surrounded by death—he lives it every day.

JOE PAOLUCCI: INVESTMENT BANKER

The world is filled with gay lawyers, and Joe Paolucci knows a number of them. He does not, however, know any gay lawyers who work, as he does, in the investment banking world.

The 38-year-old serves as vice president and general counsel of Equity Group Investments LLC, a Chicago-based private investment firm best known for its work with billionaire financier Sam Zell. The work is as rarefied as it sounds. It is, Joe says, "a very white, very macho business. A lot of gay men are not attracted to something like this. In fact, you rarely see gay corporate lawyers in general. It's very combative work, a lot like playing sports. It's almost like being back in high school. You have to be assertive and controlling over a lot of straight men, guys who have always acted the same way. One guy keeps a picture of himself in his football gear over the credenza in his office. It's definitely not the type of environment that attracts gay men."

However, Joe moves easily in this hyper-straight world that he entered without thinking about the consequences of being a gay man. He always knew he lacked the patience necessary to enter academia or another white-collar field. He had always enjoyed "playing ball" on other men's turf. And quite frankly, he adds, the money is great.

Like many successful, high-powered people, Joe came from a less privileged background. As newlyweds in 1958, his parents immigrated to the United States from Italy. His father, a tailor, provided a middle-class upbringing. Joe graduated in 1981 as the valedictorian of Illinois's Joliet West High School, then entered the prestigious University of Chicago. In 1986 he earned his master of business administration degree from the same school's Graduate School of Business. Three years later Cornell University awarded him a law degree.

He took his first job with a large Chicago law firm specializing in mergers and acquisitions. Two years later he moved to another one in the same city. In 1996 he joined a third law firm, where 40 attorneys and paralegals worked solely on Sam Zell's portfolio. Within a few months Joe was named vice president. He focused on corporate securities work, buying and selling companies.

In the summer of 1999 the firm dissolved. Nearly every lawyer left. Joe was one of only two who remained. Since then, his work has expanded to include making initial decisions about the structure of business transactions, negotiating major terms, drafting letters of intent, and hiring outside legal firms to hammer out details while he helps manage the broader process.

Such work requires Joe to think on his toes: Passive corporate attorneys get eaten alive. "The law is not a genteel profession," he says bluntly. "This is an aggressive business. You can never show you're worried about a problem. You need a poker face. You have to solve problems on the spot and deal with a lot of issues simultaneously. I manage maybe six deals at once, making investments on behalf of Sam and his family, and I also handle litigation. It's high-stress, high-stakes, very entrepreneurial, and very intense."

The best part of Joe's job, he says, is the chance to work with colleagues he likes. They are bright, sophisticated, dedicated, interesting, and fun; they also get along well with each other. Eight people comprise Joe's corporate-equity investment group. Most are former investment bankers. All come from excellent schools. Each somehow caught Sam Zell's eye and was hired to work full-time for him. Seven are white; the newest member is black. All except Joe are straight.

"These are Type AAA personalities," he says. "Everyone is 'on' all the time. There's a lot of jock fraternity types between the ages of 29 and 37. Some of them have no children, and those who do have very young kids."

Equity Group Investments is the first firm at which Joe has been out. Though his previous two jobs were only a few years ago, he says that was a different time entirely. The rise in news coverage of topics like domestic-partner benefits, civil unions, and gay adoption, along with the boom in gay-themed movies and TV shows, has primed colleagues to understand that, beneath its veneer of homogeneity, a corporate law office might include a bit of diversity after all.

As a fledgling lawyer a little over a decade ago, Joe feared that coming out would block his route to the top. He recalls the day a man sat for an interview with Joe and several senior partners. The man had barely left the room when two attorneys began talking loudly about his presumed homosexuality. Joe felt he had to remain silent. The incident made an enormous and negative impression on Joe.

Soon after joining his second firm, Joe knew he did not want to become a partner there. Recognizing that he would be leaving shortly, he found no reason to bring up his sexuality. He was also deterred by the experiences of two out attorneys. "The situation did not work out well," Joe says cryptically.

It did not take long to realize that working for Sam Zell was a great career move. The financier—a brilliant, quirky man who worked in jeans and a goofy sweater as far back as the '70s, when no one else did—inspired Joe to do his best professional work. The only way that was possible, Joe says, was to be out.

Two months after joining the firm, Joe was sent to Milan to look at an Italian motorcycle company Sam was thinking of buying. Several senior partners went too, in addition to a young investment banker and attorney. Joe's game attempts at speaking Italian impressed them, and the group grew close. One night Joe asked a colleague if he'd ever had gay friends. The man replied that he had known gay people all his life.

Hours later, at 4 A.M.—the group stayed up so they could sleep on the plane—Joe came out to a member of the group. The man said his brother-in-law was gay. From that moment on Joe treated his homosexuality "casually."

He gathered the courage to take his partner, Tom, a solo practitioner specializing in bankruptcy law, to company events. Doing so was scary at first. "The reality of something like that is always more difficult than the concept," Joe says. But such situations soon felt comfortable. Now Joe and Tom invite his corporate group to their annual Christmas party, where most of the 150 guests are gay men. Coworkers often comment that Joe's holiday bashes are a lot livelier than straight parties.

Joe and Tom also invite company lawyers and their spouses to a summer party. One man, an Orthodox Jew who was both the most recent hire and a new father, seemed petrified to accept. However, he walked all the way to the Sabbath gathering and got through the day. Joe ended up as the man's mentor, a situation he says has worked well for both.

Joe is proud that, from early in his career at the firm, he placed his sexuality on the table. "I showed my house and my spouse to everyone," he says. "If you don't, then you're a big mystery, and everyone talks." And that is not a good recipe for business success.

Even in corporate law offices, however, personal life sometimes intrudes beyond casual conversation. In summer 1998 Joe told colleagues that he and Tom were adopting a child. Gay fatherhood was still a new concept, but because he would be taking three trips to Eastern Europe and a two-month leave of absence, Joe wanted to be up front. Many coworkers reacted first with surprise—"They're bright, but they just didn't know gay men could have kids," he explains—and then later, when the couple actually adopted identical twin boys, with shock. Part of the reaction, Joe admits, could have arisen because he and Tom had never been known even to baby-sit.

Soon after Joe returned to work, a senior attorney asked him to attend a meeting. He followed her down the hall only to find three dozen lawyers, bankers, and accountants crammed into a conference room. They were throwing a surprise baby shower, complete with presents from individuals and the firm.

A few weeks later, when Joe and Tom sent out adoption announcements, they received a number of thoughtful gifts. The best came from straight colleagues. "Gay guys don't know what to do about kids," he says wryly. "It's not part of their psyche. Or maybe they're just scared."

Having children has helped Joe bond with the straight men in his office—including another new father of twins. As a dad, Joe's favorite topics of conversation are preschools, age-appropriate videos, and kid-friendly weekend activities. Previously, he notes, he excluded himself from casual office banter. "These guys talk about sports constantly. My God, they just yammer on about baseball teams I've never heard of. Now I've got things of my own to say."

Adopting twins has helped him grow closer with men in the office outside of work too. They share occasional dinners and get-togethers at a local playground or zoo. Recently he and a group of colleagues, spouses, and children ate at a noisy large restaurant. Joe's twins behaved badly, with one kicking a full glass of beer into the lap of the only single, childless man there. In an ironic role reversal, Joe worried that incident might give the man a negative impression of all children and parents.

"I can't express how important it is to build these kinds of bonds with coworkers," he says. "And none of it would have been possible for me if I wasn't out. I've been able to create a level of trust, confidence, kinship, and understanding with my coworkers that is invaluable. No one trusts a mystery."

For so many reasons Joe feels much better today than he did at his first job a dozen years ago. "I really hit my potential by coming out," he says. "I used to be too reserved, not confident enough. It held me back. I think that's a mistake many gay men make."

He is displeased, however, that so few attorneys are out, even in as gay-friendly a city as Chicago, and he is disappointed his firm does not offer domestic-partner benefits. "We do have antidiscrimination language, but even though I've tried, I've never been given a real reason for not having benefits," he says. "But Sam owns the firm, and he does what he wants. He's been very good to me, and I'm not really complaining. I understand it's his decision even though I think it's the wrong one."

So what will it take for Joe Paolucci to no longer be the only out gay investment banking attorney in Chicago? "I think society is already there," he says. "And I think the opportunity is there. People just have to go out and look for opportunities to do it. We—gay people—are not going to be invited in to the party. We have to come in ourselves. There's a lot of money to be made in this business, and we shouldn't limit our opportunities just because we think or fear something bad may happen if we're honest."

ERIC McCARTY: CAR SALESMAN

It is unlikely that on the day a young man announces that he wants to be a car salesman, an anguished mother has ever cried, "Oh, why couldn't you have told me anything else? I would rather hear you say you were gay than a car salesman!"

Unlikely—but not far from the truth. Of the thousands of jobs one can take in this world, few rank lower in terms of respect and prestige. Car salesmen—and, much to feminists' delight, they are still virtually all men—are stereotyped as poorly dressed, fast-talking, dim-witted liars and cheats out to separate car buyers from their money by whatever means necessary. They have the scruples of Eddie Haskell, the brains of Beavis, and most of the time they act like buttheads.

It is not the type of work environment likely to attract gay men. Many grow up feeling marginalized enough in their families and at school; they don't need to find a profession that society looks down on too.

Then again, some gay men love cars. They enjoy learning about them, being around them, even selling them. Car dealerships are as natural and comfortable a place for those men as Fire Island is for circuit queens.

Eric McCarty is one such gay man. He is completely out at the large Pittsburgh-area Volkswagen and Subaru dealership where he works. He has had his ups and downs, but he expected his openness would pay off in at least one way: Gay and lesbian customers would flock to buy automobiles from one of their own.

That never happened. In fact, in nearly seven years on the show-room floor Eric sold exactly one vehicle because he was gay. "The treatment car salesmen get from customers is abysmal," he says. "It's impossible to conceive of being treated more poorly. They treat you like you're lying to them, and then they expect you to tell the truth. You can sell them six great cars, and they leave you for someone who will sell them the seventh for $50 less. It's a ridiculous relationship."

That dysfunctional relationship is one reason Eric recently changed job titles. He is now a sales and leasing consultant at the same company. His job is to greet customers, find out what is wrong with their vehicles, then get them fixed. It is customer service, not customer sales, which seems far better suited to a man who enjoys interacting with people. But oh, the stories he can tell from his days as a car salesman.

Eric, who grew up in small-town Indiana, was not out at his first job, a tractor supply company. "It was farm country. The Muzak they played was country. Being out didn't seem wise," he explains. He did come out at his next workplace, Kentucky Fried Chicken. Just 23, he was named manager of three stores. When he was called "faggot," he replied, "Yes, I am." That honesty and the fact that he did not make a big deal of his homosexuality—he simply lived his life as he always had and talked about his relationships the same way his straight colleagues did—earned him the grudging respect of both his bosses and employees. "If it wasn't for me, some of them might never think they knew a gay person," he says. "But they dealt with it well, and I miss them."

Yet Eric has always been more fascinated by cars than fried chicken, and in April 1993 he began selling automobiles. In an industry notorious for Saturday sales, he was fortunate to be able to attend that month's March on Washington for lesbian, gay, and bisexual rights. He returned to work the following Monday with a fierce sunburn. He told his new coworkers he had been "out with friends," which was true on several levels, but did not realize he had been shown on the evening news carrying the Pennsylvania banner. No longer did Eric have to worry about coming out at work; he already was.

The reaction was not always positive. One day someone scrawled "fag" on his time card. Eric told the office manager to put the card in his file as a permanent record. Some mechanics have not treated him well. Eric understands: Few have much exposure to gay people. One mechanic had a brother who died of AIDS, but instead of acting like an ally, that man went out of his way to treat Eric poorly. Eric was hurt but never followed up. He figured the mechanic had issues he needed to work out on his own.

Just as he had at KFC, Eric tried to let his colleagues know he was no different from them. When they ogled women, he ogled the women's boyfriends. It was his own special way of breaking down barriers: He acted like himself.

Of course, being gay at sales meetings is one thing; being out to customers who walk into the showroom is entirely different. But in the cutthroat car business one seizes any advantage he can, and for two years Eric advertised in the local gay press. It was an expensive undertaking, yet in all that time his ads netted him only one sale. "People buy cars from companies that are gay-friendly—and Volkswagen and Subaru are two of the gay-friendliest, they really want our business—but they don't buy cars from gay salesmen," he says. "When I saw a gay person driving a VW or Subaru and asked why they didn't buy from me, they said something like 'You're too far away.' They travel miles and miles to gay restaurants and gay bookstores, but they won't travel to the gay car salesman. That sort of sums up the relationship most people have with their car salesman: It's not very strong. We don't really figure into most people's thinking."

On the other hand, he knows of people who walked into the dealership and specifically avoided him because he is gay. And one man, who did not know Eric was gay, told him that after six Volkswagens, he would never buy another. The reason: The company had advertised on *Ellen*. Eric summarizes: "I got no advantage for being gay, and sometimes I got hurt because of it."

Nonetheless, Eric appreciates the opportunity to sell Volkswagens and Subarus. Both companies do massive amounts of market research and know that their well-made, reliable, yet almost edgy automobiles appeal to gay men and lesbians. They advertise in the gay press—even their mainstream ads have a gay sensibility—and Subaru helps sponsor Pittsburgh's pride celebration. The two automakers stand in sharp contrast to Ford, GM, and DaimlerChrysler. "They know they'll sell 50 million cars, but still they won't do anything to piss off Joe the Baptist minister," Eric says.

When long hours, relatively low pay, and the distrust-filled salesman-customer relationship finally grew too much for Eric, he moved into customer service. Being openly gay continues to be a double-edged sword. For a while the men in the service department razzed one of their members because they thought Eric found him attractive (he did). The man believed Eric was pursuing him (he was not) and complained to the manager. Eric retaliated by sending him the angriest customers. Eventually the two men patched up their differences. Later Eric learned that when service department workers continued to put him down, the former complainant rushed to his defense. Eric calls the experience "strange, weird, and very touching, all at once."

It has taken awhile, but finally the men he works with are coming to terms with Eric's homosexuality. They realize his boyfriend can make him just as mad as their wives make them. Eric welcomes the change—but finds it wearying that every time a new man is hired, he must start the educational process all over again. At the same time, he understands why he must. "These are very mechanical people. They all work well with their hands. Some of them are very intelligent too. But they are not book learners. Current events, whatever's going on in society outside the car world, doesn't affect them at all. They live their jobs, and homosexuality is not part of that job. So they just don't know that much about it."

One day, Eric hopes, that will change. He knows, though, that such a change will require a massive shift in the entire automotive industry. "Everyone always talks about helping the customer more, but nobody—not the manufacturers, dealers, salesmen, or customers—trusts anyone at all," he says. "No one thinks anyone else matters. Every relationship is constantly devalued."

To get away from such negative thoughts, Eric spends one day a week in a completely different environment: For six years he has taught Sunday school to fifth-graders at Pittsburgh's East Liberty Presbyterian Church. He is not out to his students, but his sensitive, gay-supportive director has always known. The two have an understanding: Eric does not talk about homosexuality, but neither does he use the terms "husband" and "wife." His students hear about "spouses" and "partners." "I'm sure we've got gay kids," he says, "but in fifth grade we don't talk about sex of any kind to any kids."

He does, however, enjoy any chance to educate. On Sundays he teaches fifth-graders the story of Bath-sheba and David; the rest of the week he teaches car buyers what a crank seal is and why it's leaking—and car salesmen and mechanics that his life is just as valid and interesting (or dull) as theirs. Like selling cars, it's a thankless job. But someone's got to do it. Even on his least enjoyable or productive days, Eric McCarty is glad it's him.

JONATHAN CAPEHART:
EDITORIAL WRITER

In early 1995 New York *Daily News* editorial writer Jonathan Capehart wrote an op-ed piece for his paper about his city's gay bathhouses. He linked a resurgence in unsafe sex there with a rise in HIV transmission. Soon the tabloid's editorial pages were filled with pieces imploring Mayor Rudy Giuliani to shut down the gay sex clubs. By spring, three had been shuttered. While some gay community members applauded the news, many were outraged. The controversy spread all the way to *60 Minutes*.

Jonathan's piece, called "Getting Undressed, Going Undercover," provided graphic examples of bathhouse behavior. "Walking the halls is an endurance test," he wrote. "The sound of water in the shower room draws men like a dinner bell on a dude ranch. An attendant opens the door, says 'No sex in the sauna,' then goes on his way." Nowhere in the story did Jonathan indicate that he himself is gay.

That fact was widely known in New York's gay community, though. He had been out since his sophomore year at Carleton College. He was out at a succession of post-graduation jobs in Minnesota and New York that included assistant to the president of Carleton, assistant to the president for external affairs at municipally owned radio station WNYC, and researcher at NBC's *Today* show.

Jonathan brought three important perspectives—gay, black, and young—to the *Daily News* editorial board. All were important to "New York's Hometown Newspaper" in its eternal battle for readers in an increasingly diverse city.

So Jonathan was not surprised the day that freelance writer David France greeted him at the YMCA, where both regularly swam. David's smile belied his words—he called Jonathan's op-ed story "the single most homophobic piece I've seen in five years"—then added that he was writing a piece on the bathhouse controversy for *Poz,* a magazine aimed at men and women with AIDS and HIV, and asked if they could talk.

Over dinner a few days later, David asked Jonathan if he thought their Y was any different from a sex club.

"Well," Jonathan replied, "the Y is a *gym.*"

"Come on," David countered, "you've never seen anyone having sex there?"

Jonathan described the only time he was approached—he was drying his hair and rebuked the man—and the conversation moved on to other subjects. It was, Jonathan remembers, a pleasant 2½-hour conversation.

So he felt stunned and betrayed a few weeks later when David's story appeared. The lead paragraph read: "At the YMCA after a swim, Jonathan Capehart, naked, frequently lingers under the wall-mounted driers and observes men beckoning from the adjacent toilet stall. 'I assume something's happening,' he says coyly. From the same vantage point, just a few feet from a sign banning 'sexual activity of any kind,' he can also gaze into the large shower room and the sauna, where furtive sex is not uncommon. But before last January 31, when he went to a gay bathhouse in Manhattan, the handsome and bright 27-year-old with a cautious smile says he'd never entered a sex club. He took his boyfriend." The piece was several thousand words long. Clearly David France did not think shutting New York's bathhouses was a good idea.

"I flipped out," Jonathan says. "I panicked. I was so angry at this guy who attacked me not on the points I had made but in an emotional, irrational way." He asked his editors if he could write a strong op-ed piece in reply. Very calmly they said no. They advised him to let the controversy die.

Jonathan phoned several gay writer friends, men who had endured scathing criticism themselves. Michelangelo Signorile told him bluntly: "Grow up. You write this stuff, things like that will happen. Deal with it."

Those few words, Jonathan says, hit him like Cher's slap in *Moonstruck*. He realized with a start that he could never please everybody. Furthermore, as he listened closely to the voices in the gay community, he understood that many people agreed with him. They might never say so publicly, he came to learn, but they read his words and nodded silently.

That was one of the most important lessons of Jonathan's career. For his next five years on the *Daily News* editorial board Jonathan's attitude was: "OK—all these people agree with me, yet no one is willing to step forward and say so. I guess that makes it my mission to speak for everyone too afraid to poke his head over the foxhole for fear of being shot." And although he is no longer a newspaper editorial writer—in mid 2000 he joined Bloomberg News as a national affairs columnist—he retains that same philosophy. After all, Jonathan chuckles, Bloomberg's audience is heavily Republican. His mandate there is no different from the *Daily News:* Be provocative, make people think, and occasionally piss them off.

It is an unlikely role for such a soft-spoken man. He lives a quiet, low-key life—as quiet and low-key as possible for one of the best-known gay journalists in media-saturated New York City—with his partner of nine years, architect Giuseppe Lignano.

Jonathan's route to provocative gay spokesperson began unremarkably. He spent the first 10 years of his life in Newark, N.J., then moved to suburban Hazlet, which he considers his hometown. He knew he was different at age 10 but was unsure how or why. Two years later, reading a religious book at an uncle's house in Virginia, he understood exactly what that difference was. "Oh, that's me!" he recalls of his reaction to seeing information about homosexuality in print. He came out several years later, as a sophomore in college, guided by a good friend whom he calls "Mr. Gay Carleton."

The political science major enjoyed his first full-time jobs, and when in 1993 the *Daily News* called—his name had been recommended as a young person who could write—he said he was not interested. However, his boyfriend and mother told him he was crazy to turn down such an opportunity, and he reconsidered. The paper pitched the position as a great place to learn political writing. When Jonathan listed the reasons he wanted to stay at NBC—free international phone calls, a television at his desk, a car to take him home at night—he realized they were frivolous.

His first job at the *Daily News* was called "reporter with the editorial board," but within a week he was actually writing editorials. "That had nothing to do with my ability," he says. "It was more about their need for writers." After six months he was named an editorial writer. His task was to help form his newspaper's editorial position. Every morning he and six colleagues pored over a number of newspapers, analyzed the news of the day, then met to discuss which topics to address on the slim left-hand column of the editorial page and in what way. The editorial board often met with political candidates—from the presidency on down—asking probing questions about their philosophies and dreams. The aim of the editorial page, Jonathan says loftily, is to make the city and country a better place in which to live.

Mortimer Zuckerman served then, as he does now, as the newspaper's chairman and copublisher. His key issues—ones the editorial board made sure they always consulted him on—were political endorsements and Middle East policy. The rest of the time, Jonathan says, the seven members hashed out issues together, knowing that while the boss would have the final say, he tended not to interfere.

The *Daily News*'s editorial position is considered pragmatically middle-of-the-road. The paper is flanked in New York by the nationally oriented *Times* on the left and the often-rabid *Post* on the right. Jonathan's paper prides itself on studying each situation on a case-by-case basis and letting the facts dictate the editorial position. Generally, he says, the *Daily News* is slightly left of center on social issues, somewhat right of center on fiscal ones. Jonathan notes that because no one is ever sure where the editorial writers will land, the paper exerts a good amount of influence in the nation's largest city.

On gay issues, Jonathan says, the *Daily News*'s record is very good. The paper came out against President Clinton's "don't ask, don't tell" military policy. Following Matthew Shepard's murder, it urged the federal government to pass a strong hate-crimes law. The paper often editorialized for New York's state legislature to enact a hate-crimes bill of its own.

However, for years Jonathan has been peeved that many gay people have no idea the *Daily News* stands in their corner. It irks him to attend social events filled with gay men and lesbians, knowing that virtually none of them read his gay-positive editorial that very morning. "People think it's this right-wing tabloid," he says with as much annoyance as he ever allows to creep into his voice. "They confuse it with the *Post*. Most gay people don't read the *Daily News*, so they always asked me, 'How can you write for those guys? Aren't they really conservative?' "

He did not help his cause, he admits, with his call to close down the city's gay bathhouses—a crusade that began with a signed column on the op-ed page, then continued with unsigned editorials. Jonathan was labeled a neoconservative, a traitor to the community, even a self-hating gay man.

"I saw it not as a pro- or antigay issue but as a case where businesses were profiting from a situation where they knowingly allowed people to put their health at risk," he explains calmly. "People in the gay community saw it as an attack on 'gay culture.' Well, I'm a gay person, and I don't see sex clubs as part of *my* culture."

The controversy dogged Jonathan for over a year, and he did little to stem it. He continued to pen strong editorials warning of connections between increases in unsafe sex and a second wave of HIV infections.

Under Jonathan's direction, the *Daily News* also criticized Gay Men's Health Crisis, New York's preeminent AIDS organization, for its sponsorship of the Morning Party. That too provoked controversy. Jonathan became even more unpopular in certain segments of the gay community. But by then he had taken Michelangelo Signorile's advice to heart and did not let the barbs sting. "The more I wrote, the more I heard from people who agreed with me, who said they also could not understand GMHC putting on a circuit party that trafficked in exactly the type of thing they said they were trying to prevent."

Despite Jonathan's leading role in producing gay-themed editorials, he never believed he was the newspaper's sole "gay voice," nor did he feel pressured to come up with "the gay editorial." He always knew he had straight allies on the editorial board. For example, after carefully reading a *New York Times* story detailing the number of gay service members drummed out of the military due to "don't ask, don't tell," he decided it was not something the *Daily News* needed to address editorially. Yet at the regular morning meeting a straight colleague raised the issue. "Boom!" Jonathan says. "It was our editorial the next day, and I didn't have to write it. That was great progress."

However, he realizes he brought twin identities to each editorial board meeting: gay and black. During crises involving black men such as Amadou Diallo, Patrick Dorismond, and Abner Louima—all shot or brutalized by New York City police officers—Jonathan felt compelled to explain that he too was terrified of random encounters with the NYPD because he knew something similar could happen to him. Similarly, after Matthew Shepard was killed, Jonathan verbalized the fear every gay man feels at some point in life. "On that editorial board, who you are helps explain how you view the world," he explains. "Whether you are a Catholic female or a young gay black man, you bring that to the table. For me, the key issue is discrimination. And whether it's discrimination based on race or sexuality, I'm equally fervent in the belief we have to root this cancer out."

He calls his seven years at the paper a very positive experience. "The *Daily News* editorial board is a nurturing environment. You can't sit in those meetings and talk about the important issues of the day without bringing your own experiences into it. You can't be silent, you can't not raise your voice and defend your constituencies' beliefs, honors, and reputation. And no one else in that meeting expects or wants you to be silent either."

The rest of his paper is a different story, Jonathan acknowledges. Assignment editors often shied away from "gay stories" or failed to include a gay angle in a feature piece. While the *Times* ran at least one gay story a day—almost always fair and balanced—and even the shrilly conservative *Post* strove for imaginative pieces (they once covered a wedding of two lesbian policewomen in Central Park), the news pages in "New York's hometown newspaper" sometimes failed to reach out to every hometown person. "I don't think it was done out of animosity," Jonathan says. "I think it was more out of fear or puzzlement of how [straight] readers would react. A lot of it was just ignorance."

Jonathan's career at the *Daily News* came at a time when newspapers across the country were increasingly noticing gay and lesbian issues. Topics such as gay marriage, hate crimes, domestic-partner benefits, and gays in the military and Boy Scouts received unparalleled attention. At the same time, more and more journalists were coming out in their newsrooms. Jonathan is an active member of a professional association that is in large part responsible for many of those changes: the National Lesbian and Gay Journalists Association, an organization of nearly 2,000 members, formed in 1990.

The NLGJA has endured its share of controversy. Media observers, including some gay journalists, have questioned whether there is a place in the ostensibly objective news industry for such a "special interest group." "The organization doesn't look only for 'good' coverage of the gay community," Jonathan counters. "We're concerned with getting fair and accurate coverage. People think the NLGJA is a PR agency for the gay community, but that's not true. We work within the media to bring about change." He cites the *Times* as a prime example. Ten years ago, Jonathan says, the national paper of record was not particularly hospitable to gays and lesbians, either in its newsroom or on its pages. Today, the *Times* boasts more NLGJA members than any other paper and runs so many gay-themed articles, Jonathan jokes, "At times you think it's the *New York Blade*."

But Jonathan's crowning achievement at the *Daily News* had nothing to do with homosexuality. In 1998 he and editorial board colleague Michael Aronson wrote 14 editorials about the financial mismanagement threatening Harlem's historic Apollo Theatre. The paper's crusade did not spare New York's influential black leadership, including U.S. congressman Charles Rangel and former Manhattan borough president Percy Sutton. This time it was the black establishment that fired back at Jonathan. As with the gay bathhouse contretemps, he learned that a substantial number of people in the community agreed with him but would never admit it publicly.

The editorial series earned Jonathan and his colleagues the 1999 Pulitzer Prize for Editorial Writing, only the second time in the newspaper's history it had been honored in that category. It was a remarkable achievement for someone so young—and led, paradoxically, to his departure from the *Daily News*.

"I looked around and realized I had been there seven years," Jonathan recalls. "I was 32 years old, which was really too young for that position. I wanted to find out what else was out there. And then I got a job offer I literally could not refuse."

It came from Bloomberg, a financial network with users who care less about pink and lavender than green—as in money. If the gay community never knew the *Daily News* was on their side, Jonathan Capehart says, at Bloomberg he is writing on national affairs issues for a heavily Republican audience that probably has had little contact—ever—with anyone openly gay or lesbian.

That suits him fine. "I definitely will address gay issues," he says a few days after beginning his new job. "My mandate is to be provocative and piss people off." The man who wrote "Getting Undressed, Going Undercover" could write a book about that.

KIRK BRINKERHOFF
AND JAMES KUESTER:
CONSTRUCTION COMPANY OWNERS

Kirk Brinkerhoff

One of Kirk Brinkerhoff's business partners is a workaholic. He routinely stays at his heating and air conditioning company's office until midnight; occasionally he goes an entire day without food, believing time spent eating could be better used on the job.

Kirk's other business partner is a Mormon. (Kirk is a Mormon too, though he describes himself as "nonpracticing.") He calls this partner a great friend. Their business philosophies are so identical, he says, that they have not fought in six years.

But for those reasons—one man's obsession with work to the exclusion of all else, the other man's strong ties to his church—Kirk is not out to either of his business partners. That means he is not out to any of his 18 employees either. And, he hopes, neither his partners nor his workers will discover his secret during the next five years. At that point—if all goes according to plan—the company will be sold, Kirk will make a great deal of money, and he will be able to spend his life "in a different way."

He is not completely closeted, of course. That's nearly impossible at age 36, even in as gay-unfriendly an area as Orem, Utah. He is out to some family members—his mother, for example, gives him "awesome advice"—and a majority of his friends. Once every two or three months he heads 40 miles north to a Salt Lake City gay bar, where he shoots pool with friends.

Clearly Kirk is not the type of man to lead a gay pride parade. "I believe there are different styles of gay crowds," he explains. "There are the guys who want to be more female than anything. I don't have any problem with that, but it's not what I'm into. There's also the swingers lifestyle, the real super-closeted ones who are ashamed of everything, and the medium-closeted, which is probably the group I'm in. Everyone has to act whatever way feels most comfortable. Personally, I believe a person acts the way he believes. If someone feels trashy, he acts trashy. In my life, I want to be higher than the standard. So in business I pay my workers $2 higher than the state average, and in my personal life I don't sleep around. I think those values help make my company successful, and personally it makes me more of a catch."

Only once has Kirk unexpectedly seen someone he knew in a gay bar. It happened in Salt Lake while he was working for Orem-based WordPerfect. Both men were stunned, but managed to have a decent conversation. Kirk does not envision a similar encounter happening again; he says he knows for certain that all his employees—and everyone else he deals with in business—is "not involved in that." On the off chance that he does run into another gay man from his company, he says that "because of where we live, we wouldn't bring it up. That would just incriminate both of us. So it would be mutually unspoken about." He calls that his "safety net, in case of danger."

144

Kirk feels sure no one would turn against him because "I'm a really good employer, and my partners are good guys with good hearts." He seldom engages in casual office banter or water cooler gossip. The few times that gay issues arise during discussions, Kirk adopts an objective tone. He tries to take a stand that will not bother either side. That is not difficult; while he is an advocate for human rights, he disagrees on many issues the gay community deems important. He declines to mention specifics but notes, "Just because I'm gay and you're gay doesn't mean we're on the same page about everything." Sometimes, he says, gay people push certain issues too strongly. The reason, he believes, is that they are not secure in their own homosexuality and feel they must convince others it is OK to be gay. Because Kirk feels comfortable as a gay man, he does not care what anyone else thinks.

That self-confidence comes, he says, from his optimistic nature and his solid, values-oriented upbringing. He was raised in Denver. When he was in high school his family moved to Utah; he has lived in the Beehive State ever since. He relishes the outdoor adventure that is always so close at hand: He can be waterskiing at a lake in 15 minutes, rock climbing in canyons in 20, and snowboarding in the mountains in 40.

He always recognized he was gay, but while growing up he was unable to deal with that knowledge. So—without causing himself undue stress—he pushed it aside. His personality, Kirk emphasizes, allows him to gloss over unpleasant issues.

After high school he sold books and encyclopedias door-to-door, then ran the returns department at WordPerfect. When the company planned to outsource that function, Kirk offered to do it himself. He opened his own firm, saving WordPerfect $7 million. He grossed $1.5 million himself the first year and was bitten by the entrepreneurial bug. He realized he could never again work for anyone else— and he has not.

When Novell bought WordPerfect, Kirk closed his company's doors. He soon teamed up with one of his best employees to sell health supplements and environmental supplies. That continued for four years, but when he had trouble collecting payments from big companies he decided it was time to leave "the rat race."

A good friend was doing heating and air conditioning work for his father's large contracting firm but lacked the skills to produce volume business. Kirk and his partner offered to handle marketing and finances. Four years ago the trio formed a company specializing in new, used, and commercial heating and air conditioning. In their first six months they grossed nearly $700,000. In the first half of 2000 they doubled that.

"It's a blue-collar field, with problems with drugs and drinking," Kirk says. Most of his workers are high school dropouts or graduates lured by decent pay. Kirk firmly believes that being out to them is of no significance, and so he is not. "Over time I've come to realize that's a unique stand," he acknowledges. "Very few people in the gay community share that viewpoint. But it doesn't bother me that people don't know I'm gay, and it doesn't bother me that I don't tell them. It's not a hindrance at all. I see it in a positive sense. There's a lot of factors in this business that could cause problems, especially with me being a boss. I don't have a lot of trust in people, let's say that." As an example he mentions sexual harassment. "It's easy to see how a disgruntled employee could say anything he wanted about me. So if no one knows about me, and it never comes up, there are no problems."

Kirk separates his work life from his personal life so thoroughly that he has no involvement in any employee's affairs. He considers none to be his friends. They share jokes in the office, of course, and call him a good boss, but as soon as he leaves work, he also departs emotionally. "They don't have my phone number or address, and that's great," he says. "I never have to stress out at home over work issues."

That hands-off policy extends to his business partners. They get together two or three times a month to discuss company matters, but when the meeting ends they go their separate ways. "It works for us," Kirk says simply.

Living in two worlds demands compromises. Though he would like to bring his boyfriend to the company Christmas party, Kirk does not. Nor did he bring anyone to the firm's camping trip last spring. "I can handle it," he says stoically. "I don't have to stand up for my rights. I just consider something like that a business trip."

He is just as impassive about a recent devastating breakup. Everyone at work sensed that the normally cheerful owner was depressed about something. But Kirk declared it to be just a midlife crisis and told them not to worry. They respected his privacy. In return, Kirk said, "I appreciate your concern."

He knows that people must wonder why someone his age is not married—especially in a young-marrying state like Utah. They probably also wonder why he seldom discusses his Friday and Saturday nights. But Kirk returns to his mantra: "That's my personal life. And no, it does not bother me that I don't talk about it." Twice he has fielded innocent questions from employees—both times he responded, "I'm not looking for a woman to date right now." That nonchalant attitude, he says, carried the day.

Recently, however, Kirk has taken uncharacteristic risks. He was featured in a story in the gay magazine *Hero*—complete with photo. Didn't he worry that such national publicity could undo his years of careful hiding?

"I thought about that," he says evenly. "But in Orem, Utah, not a lot of people are gay, and the ones that are probably don't know my workers and associates. The chances of that magazine getting passed around is slim, so I can't worry about it."

Then he delivers the coup de grâce: "Anyone who brought it up would be questioned about how he got that magazine in the first place. I guess that's one of the good things about being gay here: You don't have to be out if you don't want to, because nobody else is either."

James Kuester

James Kuester's experience in the construction industry is a bit different from Kirk Brinkerhoff's—but there are many similarities as well.

One day not long ago James sat with a vendor. For a few minutes they discussed business—James owns a small steel fabricating firm—when suddenly the vendor asked a question having nothing to do with shearing, laser-cutting, or materials handling.

"Are you gay?" he wondered.

James was floored. The two men had met just half an hour earlier. Hesitating only slightly, he answered, "Yes. Does it matter?"

The vendor thought awhile, then replied that it should not. He promised he would try not to let James's admission affect their business relationship. To the best of his knowledge, James says, it has not.

But that incident got the 36-year-old president of Allied Metal Products & Engineering Corp. thinking: If this stranger figured out he was gay after just 30 minutes, what about other vendors and customers? And how about his 20-plus employees, many of them deeply religious men and women for whom homosexuality is an abomination?

It is not a question James had spent years wrestling with. Even though his middle school and high school years were filled with taunts of "queer" and "faggot," he did not realize he was gay until he was 30 and already president of his family-owned company. But, he notes, for years his dress and mannerisms seem to have signaled his sexuality to others.

Despite working in the traditional, male-dominated steel industry and living in conservative Indianapolis, James does not seem unduly bothered by being gay. He is not out to most of his employees, but neither is he in. He is simply James Kuester: a financially successful owner of a manufacturing company who happens to like men.

James admits he does not seem like a typical steel executive. He wears khaki slacks and button-down shirts—"the simple Banana Republic look," he calls it, as opposed to the Eddie Bauer style his colleagues prefer. His walk is bouncy, his hips swish, and his hands fly around when he talks rather than pound the desk for emphasis.

Most of the workers the Purdue graduate employs lack college educations. Steel fabricating is a grimy, hands-on business, and most executives—though not James—are former workers who enjoy walking the plant floor. Away from the factory those same executives socialize and do deals while playing golf and watching sports events. James, who is not a golfer and has little interest in athletics, knows he misses out on certain business opportunities. However, he notes with confidence, he is as good at what he does as any straight man.

That confidence dates back to his childhood, when he grew up in the straight world of steel. The middle of three children (and only boy), he spent a "typical middle-class childhood" in suburban Indianapolis. His grandfather started Allied Metal Products in 1945; his father joined the company fresh out of college 11 years later.

It was always expected that James would attend college too—and, even though he had reservations about it, that he would work for the family firm. He attended nearby Purdue University, fulfilling a dream that began in elementary school the day he discovered the marching band. In fourth grade he took up the clarinet in hopes of eventually marching with the Boilermakers' band in the Rose Bowl parade. "I did my part, but the football team didn't do theirs," he says ruefully.

After earning a bachelor's degree in industrial engineering and a master's in management, James left Indiana to work for Emerson Electric in St. Louis. As cost-reduction coordinator he traveled between seven plants, with the goal of reducing annual sales operation costs by 6%. It was a high-profile position. He flew on corporate jets and met top executives. James found the entire experience, especially moving to a new city where he knew no one, exciting and rewarding.

In early 1989, a few months after his grandfather died, James was called home by his father. The heir to the company asked his son if he wanted to work in the family firm. James, who had gotten a taste of the industry through summer jobs in the shop, was uncertain. In the end, however, he realized he would rather one day own a company than toil forever in corporate America. Six months later he moved back to Indianapolis to join his father. Over the next few years he and his father bought out James's aunt, the co-owner, and James became president.

Other things happened as well. In 1991 James was engaged to a woman he met in college and had dated on and off for a decade. Two months before the wedding, however, uneasiness set in. Something about marriage was not right for him. He cared for his fiancée and could not articulate what was wrong. But he felt strongly enough that he told her he needed time to sort things out, and that he wanted to postpone the wedding. The conversation went poorly, and the two have not talked since.

Always shy and never at ease in popular meeting places like bars, James threw himself into work, both professional and volunteer. His social life was limited. Suddenly, in 1995, just a few days before Christmas, two friends invited him over for drinks. He recalls the snowy evening: "A friend of this couple's, who lived in the same building, came too. The instant he walked through the door, it was like being hit on the side of the head with a bat. I was 30 years old, and before that moment I never realized I was attracted to guys. It was completely unnerving. All of a sudden my whole life turned upside down."

Surprisingly, it did not take James long to grow comfortable feeling gay. He was secure financially—he had already bought the recession-proof company outright from his father—as well as personally. "There was not a lot of risk," he says. "There were not a lot of things, short of murder, I could do that would alienate my parents or change my life."

His days were spent overseeing the financial health of his firm, which generates $2 million in annual sales: directing its sales efforts, coordinating overall company strategy, and networking with professionals and consultants to find more efficient ways to operate. Then, as now, he was not involved in the day-to-day operation of the shop, where workers take sheets of steel ranging from one 16th of an inch to half an inch thick, then shear, form, punch, laser-cut, and weld them to customers' specifications, primarily to make chutes and conveyor tracks. James trained an excellent general manager to handle the floor; he prefers to remain in the office.

Being gay is only part of the reason he does not enjoy mingling with employees. "I don't relate well to the people on the floor, generally," he acknowledges. "Their education level is lower, so I find myself rephrasing questions and comments so they can understand. I work at trying to chat and get to know them, but I have zero interest in sports, which they love. I listen to the radio so I can carry on a superficial conversation, but I'm much more interested when they talk about their families. The main thing is, their worldview and mine are very different. Try as I might, I can't see the world through their eyes. And I don't think they try, or even care, to see the world through mine. Our life experiences are so radically different. We get along fine at company picnics, and I like them, but we'll never be great buddies."

An enormous influence on his floor employees' worldview, he says, is the fact that many are Southern Baptists. From time to time James must remind them that "expressing religious beliefs, like the necessity of saving souls," is an inappropriate work activity. One man quit because it was not a "Christian company."

Those religious beliefs, James says, extend to homosexuality, and that is why he has never come out publicly at work. "I think most people, unless they're really naïve, assume I'm gay, but no one asks," he says. "I'd tell if I had to, but I don't have to. There's no reason to tell; it won't help them do their jobs any better. Besides, I think with a lot of these people's backgrounds, if they had their assumptions verified, they would quit. And that would be unfortunate."

Things are different inside the six-person office. There, James lets his hair down. When he is in a good mood he sings show tunes. He talks about dancing until 3 A.M. His receptionist knows that men are the only ones who phone James, and he never hesitates taking personal calls in the middle of the workday. "I don't flaunt it, but I don't try to hide it either," James explains. "I suspect people in the office talk among themselves about it, but they're generally more open-minded than the people on the floor."

James is out to one person at work: his general manager. He came out after writing an essay for *Out* magazine, part of a contest for businessmen to explain how they would promote greater opportunities in the gay community. The writing process helped James clarify a number of business and personal philosophies, and he wanted to share them with his general manger. She thanked him for confiding in her and for confirming her longtime suspicions.

These days, she serves as James's ears on the plant floor, a role that enables her to tell him that employees do talk about their boss. She and James chat openly about whom they are dating—but only at lunch. James still feels uncomfortable discussing such matters in the office.

Apart from the vendor who asked point-blank if he is gay, James has fielded no similar questions from any other customer or client. As with his employees, he assumes most people know. However, because he sees no reason to tell, he does not talk about the issue. He knows of no one who has refused to work with him because of his homosexuality, ascribing that to the fact that he keeps most interactions very businesslike. He notes too that "dollars speak louder than sexuality."

However, he adds, he has come to realize the importance of socializing with key vendors in order to build solid relationships. "If I have small dinner parties, it might be more apparent I'm gay than if I deal with these guys strictly in the office," he muses. "I don't know what's motivating my desire to be more social, but the process is starting to be fun."

Does James envision a future in which he comes completely out of the closet? Somewhat surprisingly, he answers, "I think, eventually, yes. I don't know whether that means standing up in front of all my employees and saying 'I'm gay,' but if there was a good reason, I'd do it, yeah. I'm not sure what that reason would be. But the more involved I get in political issues, which I'm starting to do, the more obvious it will be to people. Eventually I'll attract enough attention that it will be pretty widely known."

Despite not being fully out, James Kuester is proud that, in an industry not known for tolerance and innovation, he has begun pondering ways to create a more open and diverse workplace. He does not yet know how to do it, but he understands that his company—and the steel fabricating business as a whole—must become more proactive in hiring racial minorities, women, and, yes, gays.

"I don't even know where to go to get the answers," he admits. "But I'm very conscious of those questions, and I have them as my goal. I'm probably far more aware of that need because I'm gay. I've grown up privileged, and I've never been discriminated against. But as I've come to identify myself as a gay person, my views on prejudice and discrimination are far more heightened than they once were. I still don't know what that means for me and my company, but I'm glad I've got a number of years ahead of me to find out."

John Duran:
Criminal Defense Attorney

In 1992 criminal defense attorney John Duran represented a client against a lewd-conduct charge. The prosecutor demanded that as a condition of probation the man undergo an HIV test. John protested; the man had been alone, and there was no evidence of ejaculation. Yet the prosecutor remained adamant. "We just don't know how AIDS is spread," she said with finality.

John exploded. "Yes, we *do* know how AIDS is spread," he responded. Then, his voice cracking, he listed the many ways in which the virus can infect another human being—and the many more ways it cannot.

"You'll just have to excuse me," the prosecutor said, a hint of condescension in her voice. "I've never know anyone with AIDS."

"Well, you do now," John retorted.

The presiding judge requested an immediate break. Hesitantly, John and the prosecutor talked. They ended up, he recalls, having "a very human conversation." By the end of their discussion the attorney had opened one more set of eyes to AIDS. As he has done repeatedly since the crisis first washed over America a decade earlier, John put a human face on a terrible disease. And in the process he brought the legal profession one step closer to humanity.

In the early years of a new millennium, the 41-year-old Southern California native continues to do that the best way he knows: by practicing law as an openly gay, openly HIV-positive, politically and socially active man who believes in his heart and soul that the law can be a force for good in people's lives. At the same time, he understands that making that happen takes constant vigilance and plenty of hard work.

Activism runs in John's family. His mother worked in the political trenches with César Chávez. Like the labor leader's, John's heritage was Mexican. Unlike Chávez, however, John's family had lived in the States for several generations. His great-grandparents were raised in what is now Arizona and New Mexico before they earned statehood. "We didn't go across the border," he jokes. "It went across us."

Born in 1959 and raised in Los Angeles's predominantly Latino east side, he says, "Until I went to college I didn't realize that 'Hispanic' was 'different.' And it wasn't until I filled out all those college forms that I found out Catholics were a minority too!"

John was different in one other way: By the time he graduated from high school his gay feelings had grown incredibly powerful. He had heard nothing overtly negative about homosexuality from either his church or family—the topic was simply not addressed—but at 18 years old he felt he needed to get as far away from home and his gay feelings as he could.

To him, that meant attending California State University, Long Beach, and working "one whole county away." He applied for a job at Disneyland for one specific reason: He thought that was where "all the perfect, wholesome, all-American kids were." Little did he know: "The Magic Kingdom was a hotbed of homosexuality. I found it absolutely amazing—I still do—how many gay men and lesbians worked there. It's pretty ironic that a family-values theme park turned out to be so gay, but that's what happened."

John was assigned to shoot hippos as a jungle cruise skipper. He found Adventureland filled with people who felt the same sexual attractions he did. Because many were so open, Disneyland was an incredible and formative experience for him. "I was surrounded by handsome, intelligent guys," he recalls. "Every dancer, character, and entertainer in the place seemed gay. Yet they were nothing like what I thought the label *gay* meant. Suddenly *gay* was not a bad word; it was something good."

Energized by his environment, John came out that year. He met his first lover, a schoolteacher who worked part-time at Disneyland, at the park. They stayed together 11 years.

In 1982 John graduated from Long Beach with a bachelor of science degree in business administration. Given that background, he assumed when he enrolled at Western State University law school that he would become a business lawyer. After all, that was what people in Orange County did. John did not know that his career choice was about to be made for him, and it would not be business law.

Within months AIDS struck Southern California with a vengeance. Friends got sick and died. Their first concerns involved health and medicine, but legal issues followed close behind. Men very close to John were losing jobs, apartments, and health insurance, and at the same time they had to make hasty decisions about wills and conservatorships. No case law existed to solve such problems. Though still in law school, John was asked to help out.

In 1987 he passed the bar and opened his first firm: Duran, Loquvam, and Robertson. That coincided with the peak years of the epidemic, and, almost without realizing it, John developed skills in HIV/AIDS law. His three-person firm achieved a number of breakthroughs. The three were among the first in the area to tackle AIDS issues, and they were the first in the entire United States to file an AIDS discrimination case. (It involved an Orange County schoolteacher who had been fired.) As word filtered through the gay community that a law firm actually welcomed AIDS clients, their caseload rose dramatically. At the time, John notes ironically, other firms were firing attorneys who had contracted the disease.

In 1989 Duran, Loquvam, and Robertson lost their 1,000th client to AIDS. Many had been indigent as well as sick. The partners were overworked, overstressed, and on the verge of bankruptcy.

Despite such hardships, John looks back on the late '80s and early '90s as the most important time of his life. He realized that the things he had dreamed of in law school—making money, joining a large firm, landing on the corporate law fast track—were unimportant. What truly mattered was protecting his friends. Duran, Loquvam, and Robertson received numerous awards from the AIDS and gay communities, and John was named Man of the Year by both the Orange County and Los Angeles gay pride organizations. But that was not why he and his partners practiced law. "These were our friends," he says with feeling. "They were the guys we grew up with, partied with, met in baths. There was nothing heroic about what we were doing."

The AIDS crisis forced John to grow personally as well as professionally. Like many gay men, he had not previously been interested in lesbians or their issues. Yet as gay women answered the AIDS battle call, he found himself talking and working with lesbians, discovering shared interests and lives.

He also found himself drawn into the political arena. He spoke to legislators and their committees about the need to write or revise laws to address the new reality of AIDS. (Several years earlier he had changed his party affiliation from Republican to Democrat.) That work provoked the few negative reactions he ever encountered. Conservatives in state government called him "the prince of sodomy" and "an avowed and practicing homosexual lawyer." He wore those labels with pride, but things turned ugly when he found a swastika painted on his law office. Two months later the porch of his Santa Ana home was set on fire. That was the last straw: He and his lover moved to West Hollywood. "I could battle the right-wingers in court and the legislature and love it. But I had to be able to sleep at night," he says.

John did not handle only AIDS issues, of course. Gay-related civil rights cases trickled in as well. One of the first came in 1989, when the firm successfully defended organizers of Orange County's first gay pride parade after the city of Santa Ana tried to stop the festivities. The *Los Angeles Times* called John and his partners "gay rights lawyers," and the term stuck.

Around that time police in Southern California engaged in what John calls "a pattern of misconduct." Undercover decoys were setting gay men up, entrapping them in parks, department stores, and airports. Defending these men extended the firm's practice into criminal law. Soon John was handling criminal cases ranging from the mundane (fraud, alcohol, and drug offenses) to the first felony assisted-suicide case brought in California in 100 years.

But many of the firm's criminal cases retained AIDS or gay roots. The trio of lawyers developed expertise in medical marijuana law, which had evolved out of AIDS patients' desires to keep their medications down when nothing else helped. John also argued needle exchange cases, many of which sprang from the AIDS movement.

He defended ACT UP members from criminal prosecution for First Amendment demonstrations against right-wingers the Rev. Lou Sheldon and congressman Bill Dannemeyer; represented two lesbians subjected to unlawful genital search to determine their gender; and argued the case of the first openly gay person fired by the sheriff's department. John won all three cases.

"This was not a career path for the faint of heart," the attorney says wryly. Nor was his personal life easy. For many years he struggled with drugs and alcohol. At the height of his AIDS practice John had what he calls "a severe drinking problem." He has now been sober for five years, and most of the last 10.

By the end of the '90s almost every judge in Los Angeles knew he and his firm was gay. But reaching that point was difficult. When Duran, Loquvam, and Robertson was formed, only a few openly gay and lesbian attorneys were scattered throughout Southern California. John's was one of the first firms to be explicitly gay: out, identifiable lawyers from and for the gay, lesbian, bisexual, and transgendered community.

In the early days, before members of Southern California's legal world knew who John was, they customarily denigrated men charged with lewd conduct. More times than he can count, John sat in plea bargain sessions and heard judges denigrate "weenie waggers." At some point in each meeting he came out. Every time the dynamic of the courtroom shifted completely. Each judge knew he had to stop; suddenly the case moved from frivolous to serious. Some judges apologized. Others did not but looked extremely uncomfortable. "They knew they'd just put themselves in a compromising situation," John says. "They knew, if I wanted, I could file an appeal based on bias, and I would have a very strong case."

Slowly, the attitudes of judges changed. One day John fielded a call from a judge who needed information on whether a prisoner could be forced to undergo an HIV test. "That never would have happened if the judge didn't know I was gay, experienced, and bright enough to do him a favor," John explains. "Today, I no longer hear the 'weenie wagger' comments. Now I'm a human being. Judges ask me about my life and my work with the Gay Men's Chorus. I've helped humanize the entire gay community for them."

In 1999 John was named partner in a general-practice law firm, Duran and Thomas. Currently, only 10% of his practice is HIV- or gay-related. Part of the reason is that new laws have been written and new case law made covering a wide range of previously unaddressed issues. In addition, private industry has become self-governing. With gay issues now an integral part of management training, the demand for HIV or antigay discrimination lawyers is a fraction of what it was just a few years ago.

"That's a good thing," John says with relief. "I don't think I'd have the ability to sustain what I did 10 or 15 years ago. It seems at the time I was free-falling. My partners and I visited hospitals daily. We went to one or two funerals or memorials a week. Eventually I stopped counting. It got to be too much."

Nowadays, he and his firm take only blatant discrimination cases. Where once they fielded two or three such calls a day, today they are down to one a month at most. However, the cases he accepts are more complicated than ever—for example, a custody battle involving two lesbians who each gave birth to a child but co-parented the two children.

John points with pride to the fact that while 90% of his clients are still gay or lesbian, their issues have changed. Now their questions involve starting Internet companies or clubs; some are celebrities whose images have been posted in cyberspace without their consent. "It's pretty cool," he says. "Our people are now part of the economic mainstream—high-tech or Hollywood. They've got positive issues, and they're dealing with them as open people. It feels great to be able to help." His practice has gone from a specialized niche, he says, to a general one for a specialized community.

John's life away from the office has grown more mainstream as well. At the height of the plague virtually all the boards he sat on were AIDS-oriented. They now include the American Civil Liberties Union of Southern California; the Coalition for Economic Survival, which focuses on affordable housing and tenants' rights; and Wendy's Hope, a breast cancer organization. He points out, "My activism in the gay community got me here, but the tools I learned can be used in many ways. These days I want to serve not just the gay community but the entire community."

To that end, he is considering a run for the West Hollywood city council. "Everyone thinks of this as a gay town, but the population is only one-third gay and lesbian," he says. "The big issues are parking, land use—urban things."

West Hollywood is a long way from John's youth on Los Angeles's east side—and not just in miles. "WeHo" is 92% white, so as a Latino, he is very much a minority. Most gay and lesbian Hispanics live on the east side or in Silver Lake. Some of them have accused him of being "the voice of the rich white male," and though he is neither rich nor white (he does admit to being male), he recognizes that his experiences living on the west side and working with white people provide him with a different perspective than his gay and lesbian Latino *compadres*. Yet John makes no apologies. "When I came out the Latino thing was not an issue," he says. "Being gay was. I needed resources, and I found them here in West Hollywood. Now it's home."

However, his Hispanic heritage is as integral a part of him as his sexual orientation. Because he is a fourth-generation American and because Duran is not a traditional Latino name (except, John notes, for the boxer Roberto Duran), he has had to listen as gay white men joke about Mexican busboys, gardeners, and maids. At such times he comes out again—this time as Latino. "It's just like the judges talking about weenie waggers," he says. "It's done out of ignorance, not malice. And when I call them on it, I see the same reactions I saw 15 years ago when I came out as a gay man."

What will happen 15 years from now? Will the concept of a gay lawyer for the gay community be derided as an anachronism? No, John says, citing as precedents the experiences of racial minorities and women. "The struggles of blacks and women have gone on for centuries, and in California those of Mexicans and the Chinese precede statehood," John says. "Such battles are never quick. They often take many generations to resolve. Gay civil rights is still a new movement. If racism and sexism are not yet eradicated, no wonder homophobia remains too.

"However," he continues, "AIDS put gay and lesbian legal issues front and center. The disease forced society to deal with a whole range of sexuality concerns. Now that the AIDS crisis has slowed, so has the gay civil rights movement. We just have to take it step-by-step. But so long as there is need for the laws of our community to be addressed, there will be a need for gay lawyers to address them."

As he looks ahead, though, John Duran sees plenty of hope. In just a few years he has watched his own law practice move from sodomy and lewd-conduct cases to issues like adoption and estate planning. "If that doesn't indicate we've made some kind of progress, as a society or as the legal profession," he says with satisfaction, "I don't know what does."

Robert Estep:
Telephone Company Worker

Every day Robert Estep is surrounded by hot men wearing tight-fitting T-shirts, blue jeans, work boots, leather gloves, and hard hats. They parade through his office at Southern New England Telecommunications, where he works as a network technician, connecting customers' cables to phone company equipment.

Robert is attracted to natural-looking, hard-working men. He would love to take the guys from work home—even just one—and see what happens. But he knows it will never happen. For one thing, he has a partner to whom he is faithful. For another, he is extremely shy. For a third, he is not out at work. For a fourth, he says wistfully, as far as he knows, not one of the telephone linemen he works with is gay.

Climbing telephone poles is not a job for most gay men, he admits. It is physically exhausting work, particularly tough on the legs, backs, and shoulders. Installers wear heavy boots. Leather straps and metal hooks wrap around their ankles. Jabbing those hooks into wooden poles, they hoist themselves up high. In the winter they must shinny up the icy poles; in the summer those same poles can be fiercely hot. At the top of the pole they pull a big strap out of their heavy tool belt. Then they fasten themselves to the top so they can work hands-free.

Robert knows how grueling such work can be. He did it himself for a year a decade ago. He was the first person in his class to complete the two-week pole-climbing school. Apart from working out in the gym, that was the first physical work he'd done in his life. To his surprise, he liked it. Also, he liked the feeling he had each night crawling into bed, beat and sore from the long day outdoors. When he was climbing poles he had no trouble falling asleep.

And he loved the pay. Plenty of overtime meant lots of money.

Though he now works inside, Robert still feels closest to the installers. He could never go back to the office environment he started in, where hordes of women mothered their few male colleagues. He has no gay male colleagues—although he suspects several women are lesbians—but that does not matter.

A tremendous amount of testosterone floats around Robert's workplace, and he likes it that way. "I don't get that kind of feeling in most areas of my life," he explains. "With most of my friends outside of work, you can tell they're gay just by the way they talk or act. But this is such a masculine atmosphere. How they dress, their swagger, the way they always talk dirty…they're tough, and they don't take any shit. It's so different from a normal office environment—and from the world I see when I'm off the clock."

Robert likes the life these installers lead—and they do too. They drive trucks unsupervised, they solve problems, they constantly meet new customers, and they spend most of the day outdoors. "Not many gay people are cut out for that," he says.

So Robert is not bothered that he has not come out to his SNET coworkers. It is a decision he never consciously made. Rather, it evolved slowly, over time, and he has come to accept it as the most comfortable way to spend each working day.

"Installers are pretty dense about homosexuality," he says. "The subject literally never comes up. They don't even joke with each other or call the other guy 'faggot.' But if I was out, it might affect our relationships. We all get along pretty well, and being out might change things."

Robert does not pretend to be straight. He has never dated a woman or lied by saying that he did—not even in high school 25 years ago in rural Connecticut. He does not join in discussions about sports. And when one of his colleagues rushes to the window to ogle a pretty girl—something that happens several times a day—Robert stays right where he is.

He assumes most people have figured out his secret. Coworkers have been to his house; they had to notice his rainbow flag and the naked David magnet on his refrigerator door. In his personal life he is out to all his family and friends. He does not think anything bad would happen if he officially came out at work. Yet Robert cannot stop thinking about several incidents that happened to his partner, a white-collar worker for a Hartford insurance company. One day his car had the word "fag" scrawled on the side by a key. Soon a female colleague made up a bogus charge of sexual harassment. Shortly thereafter he was fired.

"I guess something like that stays in the back of your head," Robert says. "It's a stupid world we live in, and I don't want any trouble; 99% of the people are good, but 1% could cause you grief. I don't want any grief, so that's why I don't completely open up at work. I just don't think there's a need to make an issue out of being gay."

Unlike other men in similar circumstances, Robert does not feel excluded when the conversation turns to personal matters. "I'm pretty well-liked in this office. I'm quiet, easygoing, and I don't cause trouble," he says. "I don't say much generally, so when they talk about dates and sex I don't really join in. But even though I don't say anything I know I've got a lot in common with them. We're all getting laid, it's just with different people."

Robert's coworkers—most of them, anyway—know a little bit about Chad, his partner of a year. Robert occasionally drives Chad's Subaru to work instead of his own truck. "I think they know what's going on, without anyone saying anything, because no one has ever asked where I got the car," he says. "If they asked me, I'd say 'It's my partner's,' but I don't think anyone is going to ask. It's not that type of environment."

Robert has dropped other hints as well. Upon learning that a colleague was moving not far from his own quiet, rural home, Robert commented, "Just what we need here: more breeders!" The man laughed uproariously then went home and repeated the line to his wife.

Still, Robert does not foresee ever actually saying the "*G* word" at work. "I just wonder how it would affect things," he says. "We all get along well, and I don't want to change that. If I came out, probably nothing would happen. It's probably a fear I'm putting on myself. But I kind of like leaving things the way they are. I guess it's just for security and safety's sake. I've been with SNET since 1978—the month after I graduated from high school—and I was probably a big queen then. My first job was clerical, and one day I wore a bright-yellow shirt, bright-green designer jeans, and red shoes. Someone said I looked like a traffic light. As I got older my gayness sort of waned. I guess I never really came out, but I decided after I was in my 20s that it didn't really matter anymore. I just didn't need to waste any more energy worrying about it one way or the other."

So he does not worry about working in such a testosterone-filled environment every day. "Some of the installers are definitely hot, but I'm in a relationship," he repeats. "The hot guys—and I find the regular-looking guys attractive, not some Adonis on a pedestal—the hot guys tempt me, but I'm extremely shy. At clubs I'm never one to ask anyone to dance. So yes, I'm tempted at work, but I would never risk losing my job for a fun time. You never know how something like that could backlash you, and with all the sexual harassment stuff around today…

"Besides," Robert continues, "I've gone down the list, and most of these guys are married with kids. I know it doesn't mean anything, but still."

He thinks for a moment, then says, "You know, there is one guy who's kind of wild. He lives with his girlfriend, but he's always talking about how she wants sex and he doesn't. He's 42, and he's very hot. Maybe he's gay…

"I guess I could fantasize about it," he says, "but that's all. But I like my work, I've got a nice house and a partner, and I'm happy. That's what really counts, isn't it?"

Christopher Veilleux:
Baker, Forklift Driver,
Log Cutter, Insurance Man

Several years ago Christopher Veilleux's partner, Danny, was hospitalized with large-cell lymphoma. Danny had worked at Aetna, the Hartford, Conn.–based insurance company, for over 20 years. Christopher worked there too, sometimes on the same projects.

During Danny's illness their coworkers were uniformly supportive. Christopher's supervisor's first questions were "What do you need? What can we do to help?" He gave Christopher a four-day workweek, with a day off in the middle to take care of personal business and run errands. Colleagues visited the hospital and convalescent home, bearing Danny's beloved cheeseburgers, fried chicken, and frozen yogurt.

Danny died shortly thereafter. Once again coworkers rallied around. The funeral service was packed. Through the following weeks people mowed the lawn, did laundry, and continued to support Christopher. "Aetna is a great place to work," he says emotionally.

Aetna is also a far cry from Christopher's previous places of employment: a wholesale bakery and a company that manufactured log homes. At the bakery Christopher spent 15 hours a day with men whose sole topics of conversation were the women they fucked and how long and hard they fucked them. The log-cutting job was just as macho. There as well, a "drink beer, bang chicks, and put down cock-suckers" attitude prevailed.

Christopher's route to Aetna was long and circuitous. For a long time he had no idea such jobs existed. He was born in rural north-eastern Connecticut to blue-collar parents, both of whom grew up in farming communities. From ages 6 to 16 he was physically abused by his father. Always curious about boys but equally comfortable fooling around with girls, his gay epiphany came one day while walking home from high school. He found a copy of *Blueboy* magazine on the side of a road. In an instant his life changed.

"Wow!" he remembers thinking. "I didn't know stuff like this exists! Men with men. That's wild!" It opened up a new world for Christopher. He kept the magazine for years.

Unfortunately, in his small town in the late '70s there was no access to gay material beyond discovering it in the street. So Christopher had to wait two or three more years before entering what he calls a "dirty bookstore," where he found more gay images. His heart pounding, he bought another *Blueboy* magazine.

Nearing his 20th birthday, Christopher realized he desired men much more than women. However, the only place he knew to find them was a bar called the Salty Dog many miles away in New London. He drove down several times yet never gathered the courage to walk in.

At the time he had already worked a couple of different jobs. His first, just out of high school in 1979, was in inventory control at the same wire factory where his mother worked. The money was good, but he was laid off following a strike. He was hired by a convenience store but was dissatisfied with the manager.

A friend who worked at a wholesale bakery told Christopher he could make good money there. For 2½ years he did. However, the price was high.

It was backbreaking, physical labor. He and his coworkers carried huge armloads of dough, dumped it on tables, then slid enormous steel pans into high shelves. After mixing 33 gallons of bread at a time—over 300 pounds of flour—they delivered it to area supermarkets and restaurants. Work started at 9 P.M. and often ran until noon the next day. Though surrounded by bread, they barely had time to eat. He made plenty of money, yet there was no time to spend it. The 5-foot-6, 130-pound Christopher felt mired in a mind-numbing, physically exhausting routine of work and sleep.

Most of the workers came from Italy. One attractive man had the unattractive habit of constantly exposing himself. "At the drop of a hat he'd whip his dick out on the bread-making table," Christopher recalls. "It was big! Holy shit! It was the literal Italian sausage, big and fat. I definitely wanted to suck on it, but that wasn't going to happen. He always joked in this old-world way about fucking women. It was such an odd place to work. I was attracted to this hot Italian guy with a great dick, but he was such a pig. And he definitely would have beat the shit out of me if I ever approached him."

The bakery atmosphere was ultra macho. Women were the topic of every snide comment, the butt of every joke. Christopher grew increasingly lonely. Needing someone in his life, he dated a girl he'd known for years. They got engaged. He was 23 years old.

As he prepared for marriage, Christopher realized his job at the bakery provided no benefits. His future sister-in-law worked for a lighting manufacturer in Norwich, so he went to work there assembling track lighting. His job was to feed copper into a spline. The plastic was stiff, and sliding the metal in was not easy. Most of his coworkers were women; they found the work easier than men because they were more dexterous.

Christopher moved over to the stockroom as a forklift driver. There, his colleagues were other men in their 20s. All were straight, yet the atmosphere was good. With his new coworkers Christopher talked about his upcoming wedding.

Suddenly, three weeks before the big day, he called it off. It had nothing to do with being gay, he says. Rather, he learned his fiancée had lied to him about her health and job. It was a difficult time. His mother sided with the jilted bride—her first reaction was "What am I supposed to do with my dress?" ("What am I supposed to do about my happiness?" Christopher countered.) He did, however, receive sympathy from his aunts and uncles on his mother's side.

When he told his fellow forklift operators about the canceled wedding, they reacted with support. After all, he seemed to fit in well with them. They all hung out together. When they went to tittie bars to ogle strippers, he came along. "We were a bunch of working stiffs," he recalls. "We looked at girls, but we didn't do anything. No one made a big deal if you were dating or not."

Christopher laughed along with all the lewd jokes. He never felt threatened by his back-of-the-mind fantasizing about guys. The atmosphere at the lighting shop was much less macho than the bakery.

A year later Christopher ran into a man he remembered from a casual encounter in a bar. They went to the man's home, where Christopher met his roommate and friends. They were, he says, "real people with real jobs. Real estate appraiser, hairdresser, whatever. He had a nice apartment, and everyone was out. They all were happy with who they were." Like picking up the *Blueboy* magazine eight years earlier, he experienced a stunning revelation.

The man took Christopher to a gay bar (after, he laughs, downing a few drinks at home to get over his fright). Christopher was terrified he would see someone he knew. To his amazement and fear, he did spot a familiar face: a "big screaming queen" floor clerk from work not known for his discretion. Petrified, Christopher did not venture out again socially for many months. The man never said anything at work, but it took weeks for Christopher to calm down.

Within a year, however, he was coming out. He grew more comfortable with the gay lifestyle—so far, that is, as he knew it. He had little dating experience, but mutual friends introduced him to his first partner. They moved in together the next year. Christopher was 27. His sister knew he was gay, but Christopher was still not out to his parents.

He came out to a lesbian on the company softball team. He also told the woman who got him the job at the lighting company, his one-time future sister-in-law. Together they cruised the big, burly truck drivers making deliveries. She kept his secret from everyone, including his ex-fiancée. No one ever suspected, Christopher says. "How could I be a fag?" he asks rhetorically. "I had a butch job. Gay people were all limp-wristed hairdressers."

During his five years with the company, Christopher met Danny. They lived far apart, so when he moved in with Danny he also searched for work closer to his new home. He found one, driving a forklift and cutting logs for a company that manufactured log homes. His parents, to whom he had not yet come out, never asked why he was quitting a good job and moving in with another man.

The log company was a much smaller workplace, not much more than a half dozen employees. "It wasn't redneck, but there certainly was a narrow-minded mentality about the world and life," Christopher says. "Probably only one person could have been an ally or friend if I had come out. It was like going back to the bakery atmosphere." Once again his coworkers drank beers and talked about the women they screwed.

Christopher sometimes mentioned his "roommate." At the same time, he says, "I hid behind the fact that I was doing butch, physical labor. I was hauling around 14-foot six-by-eights, carrying big tools and driving big forklifts. So how could I be a cocksucker?" That, along with "fudgepacker," was the most popular term of denigration.

One day at lunch a coworker made an ignorant crack about AIDS. Though this was long before he knew Danny was HIV-positive—before, in fact, Christopher knew anyone with the disease—he reacted viscerally. "How can you say that?" he thundered. "You wouldn't say that if you saw someone dying of AIDS. You wouldn't wish it on your worst enemy."

The room reacted with a stunned silence. His colleagues could not believe he would not join in their joke. Soon, however, conversation resumed—on an entirely different subject. The incident was never mentioned again.

A couple of years later Connecticut suffered a housing slump, and work slowed. Danny, who enjoyed his job at Aetna, encouraged Christopher to apply. He began as a temporary worker. Soon he was hired permanently. Working across a partition from each other, even traveling together for a special project, they were clearly more than coworkers. However, Christopher says, not once did he hear a disparaging remark. Their years there were special. Then came Danny's illness, hospitalization, and death, and the entire workforce rallied around them.

In the weeks and months that followed, Christopher came all the way out. He felt he had lost everything in the world; nothing could ever hurt him again. He was buoyed too by Aetna's strong corporate policies. "They simply will not tolerate bigoted behavior on any level—sexist, racist, homophobic, whatever," he says. "You know it's an equal opportunity employer from the day you start work. There's lots of diversity education."

He contrasts that with the environment at the bakery and log company but is unwilling to chalk up the difference strictly to white-collar versus blue-. "I think it's more the type of people, their backgrounds and educations, than anything else," he explains. "People who grow up in small towns tend to have small minds. In the lumber mill there was only one person I thought I could turn to. He was older than the rest of us, so maybe it's age and life experience that makes a difference too. And in the years since I entered the workforce, gays have come out a lot more too, so maybe we as a society are further along the time line."

Another factor is the attitude at the top. He knows out gay police officers who have had great work experiences—and others who have had to leave the force. "You see both sides of the coin in a lot of different fields," he says. "So I guess it's a combination of background, education, and the environment that makes a job good or bad."

Eleven years after being hired Christopher is still at Aetna. He works today as a business system–delivery analyst, supporting customer statements. It remains, he says, a "wonderful" place to work. He joined ANGLE (the Aetna Network of Gay and Lesbian Employees) and helped lead the fight for domestic-partner benefits. He distributes Connecticut Gay Men's Chorus fliers at work. His work area is decorated with a rainbow flag and a photograph of Danny.

Christopher Veilleux has come a long way from the bakery—and the days when his biggest challenge was hiding his fascination with a coworker's Italian sausage.

Brett Mathews
and "Andrew Peterson":
U.S. Military

Brett Mathews

1st Lt. Brett Mathews was a nuclear missileer who loved his job. He was thrilled that every day brought new challenges. He enjoyed the camaraderie and *esprit de corps* of the Air Force Space Command. He appreciated military discipline and order, accepting the awesome responsibility of working with weapons that could wipe out the planet. He thrived on the concept of advancing through the ranks, succeeding solely on the basis of performance. Most of all, the 27-year-old man loved serving his country.

Suddenly, on August 22, 1997, the Air Force began an investigation to determine whether First Lieutenant Mathews was gay. For 16 months he battled the Pentagon for his right to remain a missileman. On December 16, 1998, he lost and was discharged.

Brett Mathews is not unique. Since 1993, when President Clinton's "don't ask, don't tell" policy went into effect, over 5,000 men and women have been ousted from the U.S. armed forces, according to the Servicemembers Legal Defense Network. Thanks to the long-running public-policy debate, every American knows there are—and always have been—gays in the military.

But few of those discharged ever earned the top-secret clearance of nuclear missileer Brett Mathews.

A novelist could not have constructed Brett's story better. The third of five boys, he grew up on a 200-acre farm in Utah's Tooele Valley, west of Salt Lake City. His father's forebears crossed the country with Brigham Young. Both parents—his father was a civilian industrial engineer for the Army, his mother drove a school bus—were devout Mormons. For most of Brett's childhood there was no television in the house. The boys played board games, read books, and worked on the farm.

At 12 Brett was elected president of his Sunday school class. A few months later a fellow Boy Scout taught him how to masturbate. Filled with church-related guilt, he resisted the overwhelming temptation to practice self-pleasure.

At 19 he began a two-year Mormon mission in Columbus and Dayton, Ohio. He then entered Utah State University on a full scholarship from the Air Force ROTC program.

In 1996 he graduated with high honors. He also graduated celibate. Throughout college Brett had abstained from all sex—including masturbation. "Mormons believe any ejaculation except nocturnal emissions is a moral sin condemning you to hell," he says. "So I tried to dream a lot." Although aware since age 7 or 8 of his same-sex attractions, Brett had always fought them. He had a close call his final three weeks of college, when he began dating a man. But the romance ended abruptly. For the first time Brett's heart was broken.

After graduating, Brett was awarded a coveted slot at navigator training school. Brett was aware of the military's "don't ask, don't tell" policy, including the oft-forgotten "don't pursue" codicil. However, he was unworried. Proud of his hard-earned celibacy, he looked forward to a long military career.

Commissioned as a second lieutenant, Brett was temporarily assigned to Eglin Air Force Base, near Fort Walton Beach, Fla. With the memory of his first romance still raw, Brett realized he could no longer fight his urges. He found a gay bar and walked inside.

He was 25 years old. In short order he tasted alcohol for the first time and lost his virginity—twice. The experience with a lesbian friend was fun but emotionless. The sex with a male was much more enjoyable.

Brett began dating men, but very carefully. He did not talk about work with anyone he knew—or even suspected—to be in the military. But he noticed other servicemen in the gay bars he frequented, so he did not feel particularly worried. That, he knows now, was a huge mistake.

He began navigator school at Florida's Pensacola Naval Air Station. "I joined the Air Force because I don't like the water," he says ruefully. "So the Air Force sent me to a Navy base for training." He struggled for three months before gaining reassignment to the space and missile program at Vandenberg Air Force Base in Lompoc, Calif. He trained with rockets and missiles, spending 15 hours a day learning everything possible about satellite command and control, atmospheric conditions, aerodynamics, orbitry, and nuclear physics. In his free time he met many interesting, likable military men—gay military men. He dated a few and made friends with most. They formed a great support network. Life was good—until one horrible night in August.

At 3 A.M. a local policeman pulled Brett over for making a right turn without a full stop. He was arrested for driving under the influence even though he tested under the legal limit of 0.08. Brett thinks the officer spotted a gay magazine in his car and suspected he was gay. The policeman called the Air Force commander's hotline, declaring that Brett was DUI and possibly gay. The policeman, who was also a reserve member of the Air Force security forces, believed it was his duty to report Brett.

The Air Force took the young missileer into custody. During three hours of interrogation by a psychiatrist he denied everything. "I knew I shouldn't say a word," Brett recalls. "But I thought if I adamantly denied being gay, it would go away."

It did not. The Air Force launched an intense investigation. The Lompoc police told them Brett had two phone lines: one for work, the other for his gay life. Brett maintains he had only one line. Investigators were also told that Brett never attended military functions because he did not want to escort women. That too is untrue, he says. He produced photos of himself with female dates.

The Air Force initiated "other than honorable" discharge proceedings. Brett was assigned a military attorney but sought outside help from the American Civil Liberties Union, Lambda Legal Defense and Education Fund, and the Military Law Task Force of the National Lawyers Guild. All told him that, because he had perjured himself by denying being gay, he could not win. Finally, the SLDN agreed to work on his case. When the Washington, D.C.–based organization managed to stop the other-than-honorable discharge proceedings based on homosexuality, the Air Force vowed to pursue Brett's separation by other means.

He learned that his phone was tapped, his mail was checked, his daily actions were monitored, and his instructors, coworkers, and neighbors were all brought in for questioning. His security clearances were pulled, and he was stripped of all base privileges, including driving. Brett was assigned temporary work updating moldy instruction books in a small storage room lit by one fluorescent bulb. For nine months, he says, he was "literally right back in the closet."

Commanders tried to deny his promotion to first lieutenant, which he describes as the equivalent of being fired. Brett fought the denial and won. He was then transferred to a job in the public affairs office, helping plan a major air show. He was warned that every action he took would be scrutinized closely and that any public statements could be used against him. "It was psychological warfare," Brett explains. "Everything I said or did was recorded and documented. They wanted me to quit, make a mistake and get fired, or go crazy." The air show went off flawlessly, but based on a list of tiny infractions amassed by Brett's superiors, his commander ordered a psychiatric evaluation.

After a battery of tests Brett was diagnosed as suffering from severe anxiety and moderate-to-severe depression with suicidal tendencies. That allowed the Air Force to initiate new discharge proceedings, this time based on Brett's "untrainability" and lack of security clearance. The secretary of the Air Force signed off on the documents, and Brett was given an honorable discharge. However, he was stripped of all benefits and privileges. In an attempt to recoup his scholarship, the Air Force garnisheed his wages between September 1998 and his official discharge date three months later.

The continuing trauma caused Brett's hair to fall out. He developed acid reflux disease, and the weight on his 5-foot-9 frame dropped to 120 pounds.

His family, however, knew none of that. Throughout Brett's ordeal the Air Force had in its arsenal the equivalent of a nuclear weapon, and Brett understood the military well enough to believe it could be used any time: His family would find out. "That was just more psychological warfare," Brett says. "No wonder I was anxious and depressed."

When his discharge was final, Brett moved to Los Angeles, where he had a network of friends. He found work as personal assistant to an actress, then as executive assistant to the CEO of an environmental public relations firm.

Shortly before Easter 1999 one of Brett's brothers called. He said their mother had mentioned that Brett liked boys more than girls. The brother assured him that no one else believed it. Brett realized that his life was being discussed back in Utah and that "don't ask, don't tell" worked just as poorly in his family as it did in the military.

A week later Brett's mother arrived for a long-planned visit. She met his "semi-queeny" roommate. Shortly thereafter, while driving, Brett told her about his brother's phone call. He added, "It's true."

"So you're telling me you're gay," his mother said.

"Yes," Brett replied.

He cried. His mother sobbed hysterically. She pounded her chest, cursed God, and said both would be better off if he drove the car into a telephone pole. She blamed herself and her husband for Brett's homosexuality and Brett for not trying hard enough to change. For the rest of the week she lay curled in the fetal position on a bed. She read Scripture, told Brett to join her in prayer, asked if he was sure he was gay, and begged him to change. "I probably gave her more hope than I should have," he says in retrospect.

When she returned to Utah, Brett's mother told her husband, Brett's brothers, and their wives that he was gay. They demanded he come home immediately and enroll in a church deprogramming course. He refused.

Two weeks later Brett's father phoned with the news that he and two of Brett's brothers were ready to fly to California. They had rented a truck and would drive back with Brett and all of his belongings so the church could save him. They promised to help pay all of his bills.

"I told them I loved them all very much, but I couldn't deal with their criticism and negativity. I said I would not talk to them again until they changed. They kept calling for the next few days, but I wouldn't answer. They sent lots of literature, but I didn't even look at it." That was the last time Brett communicated with any of them.

"I had a 98% academic average in space and missile training," he says, his voice mixing pride, anger, and sorrow. "I graduated in the top 5% of my class—even though they dropped me to the bottom during my investigation, when they started deducting points. I loved the Air Force. I fought for 15 months just to stay in." He battled to remain despite the loss of most friends, gay and straight, during the investigation. Few military men and women care to be associated with someone suspected of being gay. "The gays didn't want to be outed, and the straight people didn't want to get caught up in whatever was happening," he says. "But I wanted to make a difference. After the first part of the investigation, I wanted to do whatever I could to make sure no one else would ever have to go through what I did."

He did not succeed. The months since Brett's discharge have seen no change at Vandenberg Air Force Base. Gay military personnel continue to be pursued. Commanders still believe, as more than one told Brett, that it is their moral duty to rid the service of trash like him. Men like Brett still want to serve their country, and their superiors still find ways to ensure that they will not.

"The military is a homophobic, straight workplace where discrimination is federally sanctioned," Brett says. " 'Don't ask, don't tell' is a failure. All the top people from Clinton on down have admitted it. But I feel like a failure too. I'll never be able to work in any job requiring a security clearance again. I can't even be hired by military contractors or government agencies."

Brett Mathews has reluctantly left the service behind. He has immersed himself in Los Angeles's gay community, volunteering for everything from PFLAG's speakers bureau to the Gore for President campaign. He is happily active but cannot help feeling a twinge of sadness when he thinks about his professional life. "My dream was to make the Air Force my career, but I couldn't do it as a gay man," he says. "Now every job since my discharge has been gay-friendly. I've either had gay bosses, or everyone has been very gay-supportive. I know I'll never work in a straight environment again. It's just not worth it to me. I loved serving my country, but I guess my country didn't want me."

"Andrew Peterson"

On the face of it, "Andrew Peterson" and Colin Powell have a lot in common. Both are African-Americans who grew up in the New York area and attended City College. Though Andrew is a few years younger than the four-star general, both served in Vietnam. The two men enjoyed long military careers yet also served in civilian capacities. Race provided important leitmotivs throughout both their careers. At times it helped open doors that might otherwise have been closed. At other times it kept doors firmly shut.

There is, however, one important difference between Andrew

Peterson and Colin Powell: The general does not want gay men to serve in the military, while Andrew is one who did.

In the final year of a career that spans three decades, Andrew's title is executive assistant in the office of the garrison commander at a post near Washington, D.C. His military service is a source of tremendous pride. But unlike Colin Powell—a man he resembles physically—Andrew has never felt completely comfortable at any of his positions around the world. As a soldier he never felt at ease about his homosexuality; as a gay man he never fit comfortably into the military.

Andrew grew up in a middle-class family on Long Island, where his mother worked in a factory, his father in aircraft maintenance. After graduation from City College, Andrew was hired as a financial analyst for a television station. But in 1964 he was drafted. Vietnam did not yet loom as a serious threat; the major worry was Cuba.

While Andrew was not happy about his new job, he was pleasantly surprised at the number of trainees with business backgrounds. His major adjustment was geographic: Basic training took him to the heart of the South, where for the first time in his life he received daily reminders of his race. A number of gathering spots off the base were whites-only. And not only was he the lone black man in his platoon, he was also the sole Northerner.

His sense of isolation eased when he befriended a young white man from Alabama who lived near George Wallace. Andrew learned an important lesson: "Southerners are a lot more truthful than New Yorkers. If they liked you, things were OK." Through his new friend he met other Southerners. Together they socialized off post in the few integrated bars and clubs they could find. They shared hotel rooms, pup tents, even sleeping bags on cold nights. "There was nothing sexual about that," Andrew notes.

Always a quick study, he earned a prestigious appointment to chemical center school, also in the South. There, he learned about biological and chemical weapons, and he also encountered more blatant racism. One day he and four white soldiers walked into a restaurant. Conversation stopped. The waitress marched them to the very back while the eyes of every customer bore through them. The women's stares were the strongest and worst, he recalls. All the soldiers, white and black, felt uncomfortable, and they left. Another day, a woman called the white man with whom Andrew was walking a "dirty nigger lover." Both he and the fellow soldier were wearing military uniforms.

At the same time, Andrew struggled with another stigma: homosexuality. The only people on base known to be gay were the medics. The assumption was that anyone in the "helping profession" had to be queer. But a man in his unit kept stroking himself at the urinal. Stimulated, Andrew fought the urge to look.

It was not as if he did not know gay people. As a teenager his best friend had come out to him. Together they went to a gay bar, where a stranger invited Andrew home. Andrew was 17 and innocent, but when the man stripped down, he did too.

His mother soon forbade him to hang out with his gay friend. "He's a lousy faggot," she said. "He'll contaminate you." Andrew's mother sounded so vehement, he did not think he himself could be gay—not even after that first sexual encounter. At 19 he had converted to Catholicism. He thought he wanted to be a priest. For that reason he did not date. He did not think about other males—not much, that is.

He spent his entire two years as an enlisted man having had no physical contact with another man. He admits to taking "quick mental snapshots" in the shower, but those masturbatory fantasies were as far he went. He was not, he told himself over and over, gay. That's what his mother kept telling him too, and she would not lie. Would she?

The Army had trained too many chemical staff specialists. Because Andrew went to mass every day, the next position he was selected for was chaplain's assistant. Through his friendship with another assistant he learned there were gay people in the military who were not medics. However, he also discovered that no one spoke publicly about it. The other assistant had many gay friends. One day, out of the blue, one of them rubbed Andrew's crotch. He was excited. Soon they were having sex. It was the first time in 24 years he had broken his personal "code." But Andrew was terrified, and several years passed before his next same-sex experience.

It came in Vietnam. The first thing he heard after arriving was a warning from the master sergeant: "Don't go down to the beach at night. There are lots of faggots in that unit." Andrew did not go. However, as night officer of the squad, it was his duty to keep his men alert. So sometimes he told them to wake up by taking cold showers. And he made sure they followed orders.

Once, long after midnight, he held a long, interesting conversation with a freckle-faced, redheaded 18-year-old from down South. Andrew invited the boy into the officers' quarters, where they clowned around. Playfully the boy slapped shaving cream on Andrew's testicles. Then they kissed. Later they found ways to take jeep rides together. Mutual masturbation was a favorite activity.

"In Nam a lot of straight guys were willing to get involved with other guys," Andrew says. "They'd never do it back home. But they never knew if they'd have sex again, so they did it there." One day Andrew gave another soldier an intimate body rub. The entire time the man stared at a photo of his wife. Married guys were particularly fond of sex with other men. They missed the physical contact, and to Andrew's relief they were unlikely to talk about it afterward with others.

There were dangers, of course. During the Tet offensive, Andrew received a frank letter from a young man with whom he had been intimate. Fearing such a note could fall into the wrong hands, Andrew warned him never to write that way again. That was the last he heard from the man.

After Vietnam, Andrew was assigned to a base on the West Coast. Because it was important for every officer to have dates for social functions, he invited a nurse to accompany him to an important ball. She flew out to see him. She did not believe in sex before marriage, which suited him fine. She soon returned home, and he traveled to New York to pick up a car. He was headed back South to yet another base.

Andrew had been made a tactical officer, assigned to train young officers. He was good with people—but, he admits, devious as well. He remembers two officers who received poor marks for leadership and confidence. Andrew told them they could overcome their shyness by teaching him while they were naked. They did—and both their wives thanked Andrew for his caring and concern. He never touched either man. His sexual encounters with officers did not come until later.

Most of his experiences began with invitations to his quarters. He and the other man would chat, then share body rubs. Once a very masculine man suggested oral sex, and Andrew consented. Yet he still did not label what he was doing "gay sex."

By this time Andrew's parents were pressuring him to marry. He reconsidered joining the priesthood, but his father convinced him to keep seeing the woman he occasionally dated. Four months later Andrew married her. The sex, he says, was good—although infrequent, because they were assigned to different posts. Still, he managed to father a son.

Andrew settled into his role as a family man and did not cheat on his wife. When she was reassigned he stayed home with their young child.

One day Andrew visited his former commanding officer. In his immaculate apartment the man showed Andrew some male pornography. Then he sat next to Andrew. His hand brushed Andrew's shoulder. Stimulated, Andrew massaged the man. Very quickly they were naked and, in Andrew's words, "went all the way." He left feeling guilty—not because he had had sex with a man but because he had sex outside of marriage.

He told himself he had to find out if that encounter was a fluke. The two men had sex again. This time, Andrew recalls, the experience was more intense than any he had ever had with his wife. When he realized he was gay he felt an enormous surge of relief.

For the first time Andrew allowed himself to become emotionally attracted to someone: an Irish-American fellow officer. Andrew confessed his feelings, and they traveled to London together for a vacation. The man seized every opportunity to stand nude in front of Andrew. By the end of the trip Andrew recognized those actions were self-centered and got over his crush. He felt pleased, however, that he had finally come out to another man.

Back home, he was reassigned to a new post in Washington, D.C.—still not the same base as his wife. Wanting to share his secret with someone else, he told his priest. Andrew was prepared for condemnation, but the clergyman's response was "So what? God loves you, and so do I." He did, however, tell Andrew that if he wanted to keep his marriage intact, he could not become involved with anyone. Andrew tried to heed that advice but felt more isolated than ever. Believing he could be "intellectually but not sexually" gay, he joined an activist group. He met a wide spectrum of people there, including many who, like him, could pass for straight. He had no idea there were so many gay men in the world.

A year after his wife returned to Washington the couple broke up. The sex was still good (though never as fulfilling as with his old commanding officer), but he was tired of living two lives. Andrew found a gay Catholic organization. He met another officer—a man with three children—and moved in with him. However, he was not yet ready for a physical relationship.

As Andrew moved tentatively into Washington's gay community, he encountered a new form of racism. He met white men who did not like black men—as well as white men who had fetishes about them. He longed for a man who liked him for who he was, not for the color of his skin. He had a hard time finding someone who did. Finally, he met a priest. They dated for a while, but the clergyman ended the relationship; he told Andrew he was married to the church.

Andrew grew more confident, yet never planned to come out at work. One day, however, a colleague asked if he was gay. Andrew's blood ran cold. "Fuck no!" he spat out angrily. To this day he does not know where that question came from. For months he was petrified everyone knew.

As his fears of being discovered and then thrown out of the military grew, Andrew decided to leave active duty. He loved the Army, particularly the camaraderie and cohesiveness he felt everywhere he served. It was nothing like his first job, at the television network. Servicemen were tight; everyone felt part of a family. At the same time, however, he was terrified of being cast out of that family. His solution was to join the reserves.

Fortunately, he found a position that allowed him to retain some of that family feeling: He was named a supervisor at a military medical center. The rumors he had heard decades earlier about medics were true—there were gay men everywhere in nursing and related fields. In fact, Andrew says, "if the military had to get rid of all the gays, they'd have to close down every hospital. It's the one place the bubba mentality isn't OK. You wouldn't believe the number of gays in the patient-care side of things."

Yet, even surrounded by gay men and in his civilian role, Andrew hides his homosexuality. "I might not be fired if I came out, but my effectiveness would definitely go down. I wouldn't be able to get anything done," he says. "This is still a military facility, and they just don't tolerate openly gay men. I'm in a high-level position, and I know I can't be out. A lot of my work depends on my ability to influence people to get their work done. Everyone has to feel confident in me, and if I came out, there'd be a significant segment that would not."

Being a closeted 50-something man does not make Andrew feel good. He hears homophobic jokes and bites his tongue. He keeps silent about his yearlong relationship. And when hundreds of thousands of gay men and lesbians descended on Washington for the Millennium March in spring 2000, he remained on the sideline. "I didn't feel I could participate," he says sadly. "I went to a Catholic service that Sunday morning, but then I left." Suddenly his voice brightens. "I did get to see everyone walking around happy, though. That was enough for me, I guess."

As his boyfriend and he slowly venture out in public together, Andrew Peterson looks forward to impending retirement. He finally feels able to communicate with his lover while at work (a private phone line and voice mail lend some help). He is even gaining the courage to come out to his brother. (His sister, a born-again Christian, is "a lost cause.")

"Finally I'm happy," he says. "I'm part of a couple. I'm not ready to be out at work, and I don't think I ever will be, but it won't be the end of the world if something happens and I am."

At last he laughs. "I love being gay, but I guess you could say I'm still not totally comfortable with it. There's a woman who flirts with me in the office and a male engineer down the hall who does the same thing. I guess he knows. But my secretary—she just wonders what that's all about. I don't know that she'll ever figure it out. And I probably shouldn't care if she does. Right?"

FRANK LOULAN: RAILROAD WORKER

Some of the men profiled in this book acknowledge that being gay has affected their work life. Hiding in the closet prevented them from knowing colleagues better, they say, or participating fully in office banter or after-work social activities.

Others feel their homosexuality has never limited what they do on the job or how they act. Like every human being they have good and bad relationships at work, but those have nothing at all to do with sexual orientation.

Frank Loulan admits that his entire life—every waking moment—is lived through the prism of his sexuality. Whether in the trains, railroad yards, and railway offices where he has spent most of his work years or in his spare hours off the job, Frank stays apart from other people. He is by nature not a backslapper or glad-hander. His aloofness is intertwined with a concern that those around him might think he is coming on to them. For decades he has striven never to place himself in a position anyone could call compromising. Since becoming a supervisor, that worry has become an even bigger part of his personality. It spills from the railroad into his social life. "I don't have an easy, kidding rapport with others," Frank admits in his serious, intense way.

He is instead a meticulous planner: an *i*-dotting, *t*-crossing man who knows what needs to be done, then makes sure it happens. He is well suited to his job as a yard supervisor for Union Pacific Railroad but assumes that in his role he drives people crazy. Like his homosexuality, though, his detail-oriented personality is not something he could change. It is simply who he is.

It is who Frank Loulan has been his entire life. Born and raised in Phoenix—where he still lives, following stops throughout the West—Frank found school difficult. And from fifth grade on, he knew he was in some way different from other boys. Gym class showers were particularly troubling. Sometimes he skipped the class entirely and was penalized for it. Because he did not enthusiastically embrace sports and games, he was called "queer" and "faggot." "I think kids can sense when other kids are different," Frank says. "And I was standoffish even then, probably because I was uncertain about my feelings. I knew they were unacceptable even if I couldn't define what they were."

He survived grade school and found things somewhat better at Phoenix Central High. He could choose his own classes, and physical education was no longer required. He discovered joy in vocal music, inspired by a teacher whose chorus was the best in Arizona. Frank was an All-State choral member as a senior in 1969.

When his parents asked about a graduation present, his response was instant: a train trip. This was not as unusual as it seems. When Frank was young, his father—a train buff who worked for a General Motors division that produced early diesel locomotives—had occasionally taken Frank to the depot. But his parents scoffed, and it took some badgering by their son to get the gift he asked for.

Frank traveled to Los Angeles, then north to San Francisco, and on to Seattle. He took a ferry to Victoria, British Columbia, and finally returned home.

It was a memorable journey. He spent late nights talking with trainmen (some of whom, he recalls, were quite cute) and decided that what he wanted in life was to work on the railroad.

But the Vietnam War was raging, so Frank enrolled in Phoenix College, a two-year school. He lasted a year and a half, all the while feeling he was biding his time until he became old enough for a railroad to hire him.

"I was infatuated by the sound, the speed, the feel of trains," he recalls. "I considered it very glamorous. I wasn't really interested in my classes, so I spent most of one year hanging around the switching crews at the Phoenix rail yard. I was also working part-time at a motel, but I played poker and drank coffee with the crews late at night. They wondered what I was doing—I was tall, skinny, unmuscular, not physically fit—but they knew I was a train nut."

Everyone—including Frank's father—thought he would tire of his obsession. But when the call came from Southern Pacific he promptly quit college.

Frank "made his date"—established seniority—on April 19, 1971. His first job was as switchman. He spent eight hours a day in the yard. He switched rail cars coming in, slotted them (placed them on tracks in the most efficient order for unloading), and made up trains going out.

A year and a half later he got seniority on an actual train, as a brakeman. That sent him away to places like Tucson and Yuma. He soon received promotions, in the yard as foreman and on the train as conductor. In 1974 he was transferred to Klamath Falls, Ore., then two years later to San Luis Obispo, Calif.

In 1980 he became a full-time yardmaster, a supervisory position. He was responsible for all yard operations, everything from safety to assigning work crews. For over 20 years now Frank has been a yardmaster.

When he was hired at 19 he was not out, not even to his family.

At that point he was wrestling with many unanswered questions about his sexuality. He had not yet had sexual relations with anyone, male or female. He spent a great deal of time asking God to change him. Frank's image of a gay person was "an old man in a raincoat trying to molest boys in the park." Yet he knew that stereotype did not fit him; he was sure he was a good person. He struggled to reconcile his feelings for men with his Lutheran upbringing and strong belief in God. He waited to grow out of what he desperately hoped was a phase. He prayed as hard as he could and waited to be attracted to women.

It did not happen. Eventually he came to understand that he was gay and would never change. He joined a group called Lutherans Concerned for Gay People.

In 1977 Arizona legislators debated a revision of the state criminal code, including a recommendation to do away with laws relating to "lewd and lascivious acts" and "crimes against nature" (sodomy). Established in their place would be a provision for "homosexual conduct." These laws would cover the same offenses as before yet apply only to gay people. Heterosexuals would be exempt.

Frank went to an organizational protest meeting. He was, he says, "young, gung ho, idealistic, and fairly articulate." He was asked to speak before the state's senate judiciary committee. He knew the press would be there. He also knew that, because he was yet not out to his parents, he did not want his picture on the front page of the *Arizona Republic* or his face shown on the 6 o'clock news—at least without their knowledge. That was the impetus for his coming-out.

His father said he never had an inkling Frank was gay. His mother cried. Over the years they became very supportive, even leaving their church over a gay-related issue.

In March 1977 Frank testified before the judiciary committee. One of its members was a legislator named Jim Kolbe; today he is the only openly gay Republican in the U.S. Congress. He and a Democratic senator from Yuma were the committee's most positive members. Frank's speech helped rally support against the proposed criminal code revision. His photo never appeared in the paper or on television.

He was still not out at work, though. In fact, in his six years with the railroad he had not talked about a girlfriend, never even mentioned a date.

At the same time, in Florida, orange juice spokesperson and former beauty queen Anita Bryant was crusading against gays. After her Tucson appearance was picketed by pro-gay activists, a letter writer in the *Republic* complained about "human scum" protesting against "the most admired woman in America."

Frank was enraged. He wanted to respond, but his mother warned him there might be consequences. Still, the young man's idealism prevailed. His letter to the editor appeared on Easter Sunday—an "ironic and fortuitous" date, he says. A clerk at work with time on his hands that day read it, photocopied it, and placed it all around the rail yard office.

In the letter Frank did not say he was gay. He merely condemned the previous writer, noting that the person probably did not know any homosexuals and, if he did, he might not loathe them. Though the clerk never spoke directly to Frank, another colleague told him, "That took a lot of balls to write. Some people might think you were queer."

Frank responded, "Well, I am." His heart was racing, but he stayed calm. So did his coworker. In fact, the man turned out to be quite supportive. A major hurdle at work had been overcome.

Gradually Frank came out to others at the rail yard. Most of his experiences since then have been positive; a few have not. Some support came from unexpected quarters. Several times he heard third-hand that colleagues he did not even know had told others to back off. "What do you care what he does in bed?" they would ask. "Who gives a shit? He does a good job here."

Two of the most memorable negative reactions came several years apart. In the '80s a coworker asked Frank to meet his girlfriend away from work. Frank, wary, did not. He later learned it was a setup and that he would have been assaulted.

Then in 1992 a switchman with a reputation for inept work habits and a short attention span transferred to Arizona from California. He repeatedly said "faggot" over his walkie-talkie. Frank told his boss, but the switchman denied doing it. He then E-mailed every Southern Pacific officer, accusing Frank of harassment and other offenses. With the help of a person in Labor Relations at company headquarters in San Francisco, the incident was resolved.

Usually, however, Frank's homosexuality is a nonissue. His colleagues and the men he supervises have been attracted to railroad work because the pay is excellent and it is the kind of work in which a person's private life seldom intrudes. Although those workers have had, for the most part, little exposure to homosexuality, they realize it does not affect Frank's job. They know too that he treats them well.

By being relatively open—if quiet—about his life, Frank has helped at least two clerks and a company police officer come out. They saw that he was well accepted and realized they no longer had to hide. An engineer with a gay son and a conductor with a gay relative both talked to Frank about their situations. He thinks he helped both people move closer to acceptance.

Although he is out at the yard, Frank has never discussed being gay at union meetings or with Transportation Communications International Union officials. He has mixed feelings about the organization. He always knew his union would stand up for him if he had a gay-related problem and would never allow him to be fired for unjust cause. At the same time, though, he realizes that union leaders are human, and he feels that they would not be receptive to talking about gay issues.

After two decades of being quietly out, Frank senses his visibility is important. He hopes new gay hires feel comfortable at Union Pacific (the company that took over Southern Pacific in 1996). He does not come out all over again whenever someone joins the yard. For years he did not have to. That task was appropriated by a man he describes as "a real motormouth who talked about everything." This person let every new worker know their supervisor was gay. "It's probably good it happened that way," Frank says. "It makes it more matter-of-fact, not some deep, dark secret. It allowed other people to talk about it even if I would not necessarily bring it up. And I normally wouldn't. That's just the kind of person I am." That worker recently retired, so Frank does not know how new hires learn of his sexuality or whether it is talked about as much as before.

While coworkers have urged him to apply for a nonunion officer's job, he is content to remain a yard supervisor. "I don't like playing company games," he explains. "And I don't know as an openly gay man how far I'd advance in management. Those kinds of jobs take a lot of time, and it's not worth the extra money to me. So I'll probably always do what I'm doing."

As he looks back on a life spent working on the railroad, Frank says he has tried to guide himself by these philosophies: "There will be people who will like me for the right reasons, and those who will like me for the wrong reasons. There will be people who will dislike me for the right reasons, and these who will dislike me for the wrong ones. The only people I need to concern myself with are the people who dislike me for the right reasons. I have to do something about that. But I can't worry about people who dislike me for being gay. That's their problem. I'm not perfect, but my sexuality is not part of that imperfection."

BOB WITECK:
PUBLIC RELATIONS EXECUTIVE

In 1993 American Airlines had a problem with gay people. Actually, it was two problems: In April a crew member requested that all blankets and pillows be changed on a flight carrying a group of gays and lesbians back to Dallas from the March on Washington. Seven months later a passenger with AIDS hung an intravenous bag over his seat and refused to cover open sores on his face as he sat on a plane at Chicago's O'Hare Airport. Airline representatives asked him to leave. When he did not, he was forcibly removed and charged with disorderly conduct.

Both times the gay community reacted with outrage. When the bad publicity spilled over into the mainstream press, American Airlines had to react—fast. Executives did the natural thing: They hired a public relations firm.

However, American Airlines did not choose an enormous company with offices around the globe and contacts at every media outlet. Instead they selected Witeck-Combs Communications, a tiny firm in Washington, D.C.

The choice proved to be a wise one. Witeck-Combs—which said it would take the job only if American was honest about making corporate changes, not merely seeking window dressing—helped the $18 billion company move from vilification to a leadership position in the emerging area of workplace equality for gays and lesbians. Under the PR firm's guidance, American Airlines became the first Fortune 100 company to organize a sales team geared specifically for the gay and lesbian market, and was the second major U.S. airline to join the International Gay and Lesbian Travel Association. The airline created a gay and lesbian employees group, a rarity in the airline industry. It contributed generously to gay and lesbian organizations and helped sponsor AIDS benefits across the nation. In 1995 it revamped its policy on travel for employees, extending discounts beyond legal spouses, children, and parents to include "buddies" of any employee's choosing. And, in perhaps its most telling change, American Airlines' Web site boasted: "Some of our proudest moments have come on the three occasions we transported the AIDS Memorial Quilt."

American Airlines might have accomplished some of those results had they hired another public relations and marketing firm. But they chose Witeck-Combs for a reason: Both owners are gay. And the two men have never left their community behind.

Many of Witeck-Combs's clients are groups and organizations working in the areas of gay rights, AIDS, and the disabled. The company donates an enormous amount of time, energy, and talent to those causes, giving up as much as 10% of its $600,000 annual revenue to pro bono work. In addition, they ask every employee—there are now seven—to choose a cause that matters to them and work for it on company time, using company supplies. That combination of altruism and top-notch expertise has created a client list that ranges from American Airlines, the Coors Brewing Co., the Cellular

Telecommunications Industry Association, and Meat New Zealand to nonprofit groups such as Food & Friends and the Christopher Reeve Paralysis Foundation. Yet, although the firm has grown nearly fourfold since 1993, it is still nowhere close to cracking the top 25 Washington public relations firms.

And that, says cofounder Bob Witeck, is fine. The chance to do good, for good causes, means more to him than the chance to make money off of bad ones.

Bob's background is that of a typical Washington insider. The city native (and lifelong Democrat) spent 10 years on Capitol Hill as a legislative assistant and press secretary to Oregon U.S. senator Robert Packwood, a liberal Republican. During Bob's first year on the job in 1976, there was only one openly gay staff member on all of the Hill (in the office of Sen. Alan Cranston, a California Democrat). "Gay people ran into each other all the time in bars, but it seemed kind of risky to come out," Bob recalls. However, he joined a gay rights organization that was the precursor to the Human Rights Campaign, and by the early '80s most of his friends and fellow office workers knew he was gay.

Despite his stint as press secretary, he lacked a journalism background. His role was "information gatekeeper, on the other side" of journalism. Later, as communications director for the U.S. Senate Committee on Commerce, Science, and Transportation, which Senator Packwood chaired, Bob was the media's first contact for such major issues as airline deregulation and wireless telecommunications. He learned how the press operates and how to handle the media hordes in order to get a particular message out.

Bob calls Capitol Hill "a grad school for liberal-arts majors to get real-world experience with public policy and the media." However, like any school, it is a predominantly young place. He was 23 when he joined Senator Packwood's staff, and today the majority of staff members are still in their 20s. "There are few barriers to entry if you're thoughtful and accomplished," he says. "But after a while you find yourself doing the same things over and over again."

Itching to move out of the shadows and speak in his own voice yet not lured by big New York money, Bob joined Gray and Co. The worldwide public relations firm was soon bought out by Hill and Knowlton, one of the top three PR firms in the world in both size and billings. Among his accounts were NBC and Pfizer.

In 1993 Witeck and Wes Combs, 12 years his junior, decided to join forces and focus on clients and issues that truly mattered to them. Their first office was in the basement of Wes's house. They have long since moved to ritzier digs on L Street, but the core of their business remains "issues that lie at the intersection of gay men and lesbians' business and public lives." As a result, the firm spends much of its time "dealing with the media, positioning companies, heightening brand awareness, developing messages, telling companies how to reflect integrity, and being proactive in the marketplace."

Longtime client American Airlines is Exhibit A of Witeck-Combs's work. The PR firm signed on only after being convinced the airline genuinely wanted to do the right thing for employees as well as passengers. Still, the advice Bob and his colleagues offered was not an easy sell. "They're headquartered in Dallas, for God's sake," he says. "A gay person from the company sat in on our very first meeting with them, but he was too afraid to come out to us until later. We can walk in and give the best advice in the world, but any company still has to work with its own people and within its own culture. The ones inside the company are the only people who can make things better."

Fortunately, American heeded much of Witeck-Combs's advice. For example, they took the PR firm's model and developed a diversity advisory council. Today, that group has cochairs: One comes from the airline's Christian group; the other is a member of its gay and lesbian employees association. (The association's 200 members are encouraged to use the company's voice mail, E-mail, computers, and office space to meet and communicate.)

The American Airlines experience proves Bob's definition of public relations: It is far more than just handling the media. The best PR, he says, involves "a constant dialogue with a company about what it wants to achieve. It's one thing to make a problem go away—it's far more important to take positive action steps based on the problem, to make it a stronger, better company."

Oddly enough, for a profession aimed at garnering good press, public relations is generally held in low regard. Bob knows why. At Hill and Knowlton he sat in on a meeting with representatives of the Virginia Military Institute as VMI tried to reshape its image in the wake of a court battle to prevent women from enrolling. Behind closed doors, VMI's leaders—"older Southern white men, more bigoted than any individuals I've been with before or since"—let their true feelings be known. "We're already taking niggers," one said. "We shouldn't have to take women and queers." As a company employee Bob kept his mouth shut, but he never worked on the VMI project again. That experience helped him realize that to maintain his integrity he had to form his own firm.

Today, five of Witeck-Combs's seven-person staff are gay, and nearly half of the company's projects are gay-related. That is possible, he says, because the public relations field has become highly segmented. Small companies make their mark carving out a niche, and gay marketing is one of the most important and sought-after.

"In the beginning Wes and I struggled with the question 'How gay can we be?' " Bob admits. "Then we realized we can be as gay as we want to be. We don't want clients who are troubled by that; we want clients with integrity. I'm sure we've lost clients because we're gay, and others self-select out and never approach us. But plenty of clients see a connection between gay stuff and social responsibility on a lot of issues. For example, even though the closets are different, there's a strong analogy between the closet of homosexuality and the closet of disability. I think equal access for all—whether we're talking about disabled people or gay people—is the trend of the future. A lot of what we do revolves around equal access."

Bob jokes that he is well suited to the role of small-business owner because "every gay man wants complete control." Turning serious, he notes that gay men are probably disproportionately represented among the ranks of entrepreneurs. "The fetters of corporate America don't suit us," he says. "We have to design our own career paths because we don't fit in. In big business you're required to go to dinners, Christmas parties, interact with clients. Public relations, in particular, was very straight right up through the 1980s. I think that's because senior management had to work so closely with their counterparts in corporate America, and that meant bonding as macho family men. Gay men, and certainly lesbians, did not feel included in those relationships. We worked in the trenches but not at the top. Now, as a gay man who owns his own small business, I can do that sort of socializing and corporate stuff on my own terms."

Sometimes that means taking on unpopular causes. Coors Brewing Co., for example, was once to the gay community what VMI was to women. For years gay consumers boycotted the beer because Coors family members supported right-wing causes. However, Bob knew the company had a good record on gay issues: It offered employees domestic-partner benefits, included sexual orientation in its nondiscrimination policy, and made sexual orientation part of its diversity training.

"They had a better story than people were aware of," he says. "They just had not been able to get that story out." It was a hard sell, but good public relations people are not interested in easy jobs. They thrive on problems and crises.

Clearly they do it well. In December 1999 the Gay Financial Network included Bob Witeck and Wes Combs in its list of the 25 most influential openly gay and lesbian executives in corporate America.

Chuck Hart: Lumberyard Worker

"The lumber business is very macho," Chuck Hart says. "It's like one big locker room. Everyone tries to be more of a man than the next guy. Everyone brags about their sexual prowess and makes exaggerated claims about their penis size."

Chuck has spent most of his 44 years in and around lumberyards. He feels comfortable with their rhythms and routines. He knows the type of men who work there as well as he knows his two-by-fours. So it is hardly idle talk when he says that Alaska lumberyards are even more macho than those in the lower 48. In Last Frontier lumberyards, he says, "Everyone talks about who has the biggest truck or the fastest snow machine. One guy here is a musher, and most of them ride snowmobiles. There's this one guy, he's only 5-foot-6, but he drives a huge truck, and he's always the first to lift the heaviest loads."

Little wonder, then, that for years Chuck fooled everyone at work into thinking he was straight. Yet remarkably, despite the hostile environment that lumberyards remain, Chuck no longer lies. Everyone at Spenard Builders Supply in Seward knows he is gay.

He certainly never planned to be out. It was not until 1997, after returning to his home state from a series of jobs on the West Coast and in Japan, that Chuck even came out to himself. Near rock bottom emotionally—he had been laid off when the Japanese economy went south; three days later his wife took off with the kids and car—he entered counseling. Three months after that, Chuck admitted to himself the one thing he had feared since ninth grade—the year he stopped going to gym class because he thought he might get a locker room erection—he was gay. He told only one or two close friends at Spenard. Not even his parents knew.

Late that summer in a gay bar in Anchorage, 120 long miles from Seward, he met a nurse. The attraction was mutual. The two men began dating, traveling between the big city and small town as their schedules allowed. One day someone from the lumberyard saw them together in Seward. Not long afterward the same person spotted them again, this time at Anchorage's Home Depot. Like before, they were simply talking. There was no physical contact. But Chuck's coworker told an assistant manager. The man—a 6-foot-4 body-builder and Church of Christ pastor—stomped in during lunch break, shut the door, and snarled, "You're not gay, are you?"

Chuck stared. He was physically unable to open his mouth but hoped his look of ridiculous surprise sent the message "no." The assistant manager said, "Good." But he paused and added, "He better not come back down here again."

Shaken, Chuck fled to his van and drove aimlessly around town. As he analyzed his situation he realized more rumors would inevitably follow. He understood he had a choice: He could spend every second from that moment on petrified about the comments, threats, and who-knew-what-else that might blindside him at any moment. Or he could tell the truth.

When Chuck returned to work he approached the 16 employees individually. He told each one, "I know you've heard some ugly rumors about me. Well, they're true. I want you to know: This is who I am."

Most coworkers took the news well. The purchasing agent "went crazy" for a few days, but Chuck thinks that reaction came more from shock than homophobia. Chuck's supervisor and most members of the sales force were very supportive. The assistant manager who had confronted him earlier demanded to know why Chuck had lied. "I told him I evaded like Clinton because my being gay has nothing to do with work," he says. For two months the man did not speak to him. He has since warmed up, though Chuck calls the thaw superficial.

Despite his assertion that homosexuality has nothing to do with his workplace, Chuck learned quickly that it does. The day after his revelation the company held a long-scheduled sexual harassment seminar. The first group of employees asked the trainer a number of questions about how to work with a gay colleague. In the second group—the one Chuck was in—no one mentioned the subject at all.

But that does not mean the issue died. Two months later the company planned a fire extinguisher demonstration. Chuck, as safety chairman, was prepared to lead the event. But at 5 A.M., on the bridge into Seward, he got caught behind a bad traffic accident. Chuck pitched in, helping clear debris. He had been up since 6 the previous morning. Exhausted, he called a coworker and asked him to take over the demonstration. Chuck arrived at work at 9 A.M.; by 11 he had been written up on a discipline form by the assistant manager.

Other slights, which he attributes to his openness about being gay, followed. Despite company policy allowing it, he was refused an employee discount on an item for a friend; then he was reprimanded for not stocking shelves aggressively enough. When Chuck complained, all he heard in response were vague excuses.

Over time, though, the problems have eased. Chuck thinks that company managers realize they might be held legally liable if they mistreat him because of his sexual orientation.

Chuck is clearly not a gay activist. But despite having grown up in and around lumberyards—his grandfather, father, and mother all worked for Spenard in various capacities—Chuck does not fit the image of someone who works there. Of course, he knows the stereotype: outdoorsy, macho, handy, and at ease with tough, dangerous power tools. "I've seen it all over, in Alaska, Washington, and Oregon," he says. "It's almost like Tim Taylor from *Home Improvement*. I don't know if it's insecurity about not knowing everything about home building or the fact that there are so few women, but there's a lot of macho competition in a lumberyard. The more of a 'guy' someone is, the more valid his status is. And that goes for customers as well as employees. People come in here looking for a stereotypical guy. And that stereotype is not someone who is gay." So Chuck keeps his homosexuality as quiet as he can.

Chuck loves his work. He enjoys building things and learning about new products and innovations. He especially loves helping customers finish their projects. He takes particular pride in treating women well (something, he says, that happens rarely in a lumberyard).

The downside of his job is that the pay is poor and prospects for advancement slim. And working in a lumberyard in Seward—working anywhere, for that matter, in a town with a wintertime population of 2,000, where the next gas station is 90 miles away—is like working no place else in America.

Being gay makes his life that much harder. Finding gay friends takes work. Recently Chuck met a gay Alaskan on the Internet and invited him to Seward. He told only a few colleagues, but later they asked how things had gone. That made Chuck feel good, but at work he remains almost completely close-mouthed about his personal life. To him, talking about homosexuality in a lumberyard still does not feel right.

But Chuck Hart has come a long way since coming out. He participated openly in Seward's recent gay pride ceremony. "All three of us who are out got in a car," he reports. "We drove through town and had a sandwich at Subway. That was it—the whole gay community in one car, with room for more." But, he says, "We did it. And nothing bad happened. Nothing at all."

The next day customers showed up as usual at Spenard Builders Supply. As usual, Chuck sold lumber to them. And, as usual, the world continued to turn.

MARSHALL MCPEEK AND RYAN MCKEEL: TELEVISION REPORTERS

Marshall McPeek

It's part of the job of being an on-air television personality: Everyone on the street thinks they know you. More than that, John and Jane Q. Public like you. In fact, they consider you a good friend.

That's great, says Marshall McPeek, for four years the reporter–weather anchor on Cleveland's NBC affiliate, WKYC-TV Channel 3. Being a familiar face enhances a newsman's appeal and propels ratings as well as advertising rates. But, he warns in the same breath, "the public doesn't know much about our personal lives." Occasionally he shares a tidbit with his hundreds of thousands of "friends"—perhaps a mention of the Halloween party he went to the night before. But chances are, he won't add that it was thrown by two guys and that nearly everyone there was gay.

Still, if you live in northeast Ohio, you would have to be brain-dead not to know that one of the mainstays of Channel 3's highly rated morning show is gay. He has come out when it is important—that is, when saying he is gay is an integral and germane part of the story. He did it in 1994 at a previous station, WTOL-TV in Toledo, Ohio, during a controversy over a story about the 25th anniversary of the Stonewall uprising. He did it again in Cleveland a couple of years later, when he brought the city's North Coast Men's Chorus—a gay group, of which he is a member—on to his morning show and talked about their mission.

"It's not, 'Hey, look, Cleveland, I'm gay!' " he explains in his earnest, well modulated, and articulate TV-personality voice. "But it is an acknowledgment. My boss and I talked beforehand. We have musical groups on the show all the time and we talk with them on the air, so this was nothing out of the ordinary. She asked if I was pre-pared for the negative phone calls and letters. I said I was, and she said she was willing to do the piece."

The reaction to the chorus—and Marshall's self-outing—was, he says, "overwhelmingly positive." There were, of course, the usual why-do-you-have-that-fag-on-the-air calls and letters, but they were a tiny, irrelevant minority. Marshall was out of the closet, and both Cleveland and his morning show survived.

Being out at work, when work involves being beamed into thou-sands of viewers' bedrooms, kitchens, workplaces, and gyms every morning is different from being out in nearly any other job. No one is more visible, day after day, month after month, than a television newsperson—not the mayor or the governor, not the celebrity du jour. Coming out to viewers you don't know is almost like coming out to friends and family—at least as far as they are concerned. They feel a powerful connection with you, and as a media professional you are taught how important that bond is to your career. So Marshall's actions in Toledo in June 1994 were unusual. He was not officially out in the newsroom—that is, to his colleagues who film, write, produce, edit, and broadcast the news—and so he was certainly not out to viewers. To be sure, there was little reason to be out. There were few gay stories in Toledo, so he could keep his private life private.

However, he was surprised and elated to learn that the producer at WTOL, the CBS affiliate, planned to run a 20-second story about New York's Stonewall parades on the air. Local stations usually leave such stories to the network news. But Marshall's joy turned to rage when he read the copy that would accompany the piece. It never mentioned the mile-long rainbow flag or the hundreds of thousands of folks who paraded past the United Nations. Instead it focused on six naked people who were told to put their clothes back on. (They were not even arrested, Marshall notes.) He told the producer the story as written did not accurately represent what went on in New York. The producer agreed, and the copy was changed.

A couple of hours later Marshall was stunned when the weekend anchor read the original version on the air. She had rewritten the copy by hand. On one level, he was not surprised: "She was a right-wing bigot who, if she had a bad night, told members of her church to pray for her." But he was too flabbergasted to think calmly. In what he admits was "a fit of total unprofessionalism," he ran onto the set during a commercial break and screamed at the anchor. He stayed there, enraged, until five seconds before air time.

When the newscast was over, the two broadcasters engaged in a shouting match. "Why do you care so much?" she asked.

"I wouldn't buy into what she was trying to do," he says about her thinly veiled insinuation. "This wasn't about me. It was about the story." Finally, however, he yelled, "The fact that I'm gay is totally irrelevant. Everyone knows! The fact is, the story is, journalistically, completely wrong." She could not out Marshall; she had nothing to say in defense. So, Marshall laughs, in Toledo he "literally came screaming" out of the closet.

He never went back in, and careerwise it was the best thing he could have done. He became a resource for gay issues at the station and a key media contact for Toledo's gay and lesbian community. WTOL's management was fully supportive. A year later, when Marshall asked to attend the National Lesbian and Gay Journalists Association annual convention in Minneapolis, they gave him time off—and cash.

By 1997 Marshall was ready to move to a bigger market. Cleveland's NBC affiliate was looking for a morning features reporter. The fact that he was taking meteorology classes was a strong point in his favor. He was out from the moment he started contract negotiations. When he walked in the newsroom as an openly gay male, he blazed a trail—there were 30-year WKYC veterans still in the closet; they watched closely to see what would happen. When nothing bad occurred, they emerged from their longtime shells. The result, he says, is a better newsroom environment for all.

How supportive has Channel 3 been? The station backs many gay and lesbian events and functions. They buy a full-page ad in the North Coast Men's Chorus program book, and they encourage Marshall to speak to gay groups as a station representative.

Marshall's influence is felt in other ways too, often behind the scenes. He answers questions, clarifies issues, and helps find resources when the station reports gay-related stories. He gave the NLGJA style guide for gay and lesbian terminology to the news director. She immediately sent it out as station policy. Being out helps the gay community as well: Organizations feel free to call Marshall seeking publicity for their causes or events. The station cannot always oblige, but Marshall's patient explanations of what makes a story newsworthy (or not) helps smooth feelings on both sides.

Of course, not every gay-related story is easy to do, even with Marshall's input. While he was still working in Toledo, a gay bathhouse opened before the final permits were approved. When the police moved in to shut it down, they beat up some of the patrons—and their actions were caught on security cameras. Marshall talked to the people involved, then explained to the news staff why the story was important. But the news director handed it to the same right-wing anchor who had focused on the six naked men in the Stonewall story. Marshall objected, saying it was his story and that no one should question his objectivity simply because he is gay. He used the analogy of a radical feminist on the staff who had never been taken off stories about women. His bosses got the message. The station aired Marshall's story, and as a result a policeman was fired.

Mostly, however, Marshall's sexuality is not an issue. He joins, and is included in, all the off-camera banter that makes newsrooms a crude place. "I don't give them a choice," he says of his colleagues. "If you tell an off-color joke, you've got to be prepared to hear another one from another perspective. We've got a diverse newsroom—including our news director, who is an African-American woman—and I'm part of that diversity." One of the news team's greatest delights is watching a photographer tread gently around every controversial topic for fear of offending someone. The man means well, Marshall says, but carries political correctness a bit too far.

Marshall realizes that his situation in Cleveland is a good one. Through his work with the NLGJA, for which he serves as a board member, he has met other gay television reporters. The larger the market, it seems, the easier it is to be out. At one convention he talked with a small-market anchor; the NLGJA weekend was a wonderful learning experience for the man—but his employer thought he was "on vacation."

When news reporters ask Marshall if it is wise to come out, he tells them to look realistically at their surroundings and the experiences of others. "Will you really lose your job?" he tells them to ask themselves. "Will you be harassed? And if you are, will the problems end quickly or stay and fester?" Ultimately, he says, each person must judge his own particular situation and newsroom for himself.

Cleveland is not a small market, but neither is it huge. Marshall looks at jobs in larger markets he would like to have and sees gay men in those positions already. He believes those jobs are realistic possibilities. "It comes down to how much the news directors like my work," he says. "In the big cities they're not antigay. If you can do the job, they want you."

Marshall has wanted to be a news reporter ever since he was 14 and playing around at the local radio station in his hometown of Bucyrus, Ohio. He graduated summa cum laude in journalism at Ohio University's Honors Tutorial College, then interned at CTV in Toronto on its version of the *Today* show. In his first paying job, as an assignment editor in Cleveland, he was not out, but neither was he in. He found other gay men at the station and socialized with them, but no one ever spoke about it at work.

His first reporting job was with WISL-TV, a small station in southern Illinois. He did not think he was out, but because he was dating a friend of a friend of the weekend anchor's roommate, word spread quickly. He learned a year later, just before he left, that jokes were constantly made behind his back. He was particularly hurt that people he thought were his friends had mocked him.

In Cleveland that is the last thing he has to worry about. He has far more mundane problems—for example, how to have a social life when his alarm sounds at 2 A.M. (air time is 5). He credits understanding friends—and an equally understanding partner—for allowing him to be asleep by 7 P.M.

Another problem for popular news reporters like Marshall is how to handle the public—especially those with an eye on romance. The issues are the same, he says, for gay and straight on-air personalities. "To be perfectly honest, the greatest thing in the world is being introduced to someone who has no idea who I am. I've been a trophy date—I didn't find out until later—and that really hurt. Some people just want to say they slept with a guy who is on TV."

Marshall's present boyfriend was one of those few who had never seen him—not on television nor on the ubiquitous billboards and bus posters that plaster the city during sweeps months. "That was great," Marshall says. "We started out as just two people."

It is always flattering, he says, to be recognized. But being recognized is hardly a good reason to date. Still, as one of Cleveland's most recognized faces—and perhaps its most famous gay man—Marshall carries a burden few others do. "To the public my face is the station's logo," he says. "I have to treat everyone well. If I say or do one wrong thing, all of a sudden it's 'Marshall McPeek, that asshole from

Channel 3.' " And if there is one thing Marshall McPeek, Cleveland's popular reporter–weather anchor, is not, it's an asshole.

Ryan McKeel

On the first day of Monica Lewinsky's testimony, Ryan McKeel passed the federal courthouse in Washington, D.C. The handsome 23-year-old had spent six frustrating months looking for work as a television news broadcaster. Now, at the urging of a friend, he was in the nation's capital interviewing for a job in a congressional office. As his taxi rode by the courthouse, Ryan spotted the media frenzy. Dozens of photographers jockeyed for position; scores of TV reporters stood shoulder to shoulder, beaming live stand-up shots back to their hometown stations.

Ryan told the driver to stop the cab. Though he had no official capacity, he wanted to join the crowd. Standing on the sidewalk moments later, he realized he had no desire to work for a congressman. His dream had never died: He still hoped to be a television reporter.

Coincidentally, within days he heard about a job opening at KAVU, the ABC affiliate in Victoria, Tex. Luckily, Ryan had some résumé tapes with him from a college internship in San Antonio. He overnighted them to the station. They called immediately, asking him to come for an interview—the very next day.

He could not make that deadline, but he did the next best thing. Ryan leaped in his car, drove to Texas, and arrived three days later at the studio. Within 24 hours he was offered a job as a reporter.

Victoria is not exactly Provincetown or Key West—or even Dallas—and that gave the young gay man pause. The southeast Texas city is a ranching town of 70,000 located 30 miles from the Gulf of Mexico, equidistant from San Antonio and Houston. Though ethnically diverse, with a large Hispanic population, there is enormous economic segregation. And, he says, Victoria is extremely conservative.

But for as long as Ryan could remember, he had wanted to work in television journalism. He had always been fascinated by news: He relished not only being informed but also the process of gathering information. At San Antonio's Trinity University, where he majored in communications and Spanish, he spent an internship at a newspaper. But his other work experiences were at television stations, where he developed a love for that outlet's immediacy. Of course, he adds, "Anyone who says he doesn't want to be on TV and become famous is lying."

So Ryan accepted the offer and moved to Victoria. His career blossomed. Within a few months he was promoted to weekend weatherman, then weekend anchor. It was an ideal first job.

Yet, as with every first job, there were work and personal issues to be confronted. Ryan had come out as a gay man a couple of years earlier. The first person he told was his mother, a chamber of commerce worker in Oregon. He had always been extremely close to his parents, and as he confronted his homosexuality—a part of himself he had managed to repress while growing up in the conservative Portland suburb of Gresham—he realized he had to share that part of his life with them too. Both parents, his brother, sister, and friends (including swim team members at Trinity, where he starred as a freestyle sprinter and served as captain his senior year) were, and continue to be, extremely supportive.

But Victoria is not the Pacific Northwest. It is not even Trinity, which Ryan describes as "very conservative, though not by Texas standards. I mean, it's not Baylor, TCU, or A&M. People here even call it 'liberal.' Well, I come from Portland, and when I hear 'liberal college,' I think of Reed."

Ryan's boyfriend at the time moved to Victoria with him, which made the new TV reporter a bit uneasy. "It wasn't a problem in terms of management at the station, but in terms of the town, I just didn't feel comfortable being out," he says. "I can't point to anything specific. It was just a general feeling."

However, he credits his boyfriend, a waiter, for helping him be as out as he was. Through the restaurant they met most of Victoria's small

213

gay community. Those were not, however, Ryan's kind of people. "Being far from a big city, it was almost a deviant crowd," he says. "Being gay in a conservative town made them be a little more rebellious and promiscuous than they would have been in a bigger place, I think. They didn't seem as grounded as gays and lesbians in a big city, where it's more acceptable being out."

Though he never came out "officially," Ryan believes almost everyone at work knew he was gay. He heard no negative comments, though he assumes a few people did not talk to him as much as they might have had he been straight.

Before his promotion to weekend anchor, Ryan was passed over once for the job. He thought it was because he was doing weather. "It's a lot harder to find a person who knows weather than an anchor who can just read news," he explains. So he sent tapes to station managers, hoping to land an anchor position. One went to KTVZ, the NBC affiliate in Bend, Ore. They hired someone else, never even acknowledging his tape. But six months later the Bend news director called offering a spot as weatherman on the 5 and 6 P.M. newscasts and as anchor at 11. Ryan did not want to do so much weather, but the job was closer to home and provided anchor experience. He accepted and joined "Z21" in September 1999.

Ryan's workday begins at 3 P.M. He spends his first two hours producing the weathercast: downloading satellite and radar maps, pulling together a forecast from the National Weather Service, and building graphics. Ryan is not, he points out, a meteorologist. But he has learned to appreciate weather, beginning with a college internship at KMOL-TV in San Antonio. Veteran weatherman John Willing took him under his wing, mentoring the young student who admitted that he did not share John's passion. "He told me, at some point as an anchor, I'd have to talk intelligently with the weather person," Ryan says. "I warmed up to it and learned the basics. I think John always dreamed I'd be a weatherman, and now I do it part-time. It's pretty ironic."

After giving the weather on the evening newscasts, Ryan takes a dinner break. He then sometimes covers and reports on a night story.

Other times he coproduces the news. After rewriting national stories, he co-anchors the 11 P.M. news (and also does the weather). He is out of the studio by midnight.

Everyone in the Z21 newsroom knows he is gay—although, as in Victoria, he has never announced his homosexuality publicly. No one, he says, thinks twice about it. All his friends in Bend know too, though not the entire viewing audience.

Being gay in Bend is far different than in Victoria. A town of less than 50,000 abutting Deschutes National Forest, just east of the Cascade Mountains, "Oregon's Playground" nonetheless feels big because of the many tourists drawn to its excellent ski, golf, and outdoor resorts. It is a booming, rapidly growing place, touted by both *Money* and *Forbes* magazines as one of the best spots in America to retire.

Gay-pride bumper stickers abound, but there are no gay bars. Despite the "deviant" nature of gay life in Victoria, in some ways Ryan found it more interesting than Bend. "Because it was such a conservative environment, there was a lot of solidarity and the clubs were so much fun," he says. "Here there are a lot more gay people, but it's like, 'You're gay, whatever.' There's not the same distinction between gay and straight."

Which is not to say it is a gay utopia. A small group, the Oregon Citizens Alliance, regularly proposes ballot initiatives aimed at banning gay marriage, prohibiting tax benefits for domestic partners, and eliminating all discussion (except condemnation) of homosexuality in public schools. Such proposals are newsworthy, but they do not bother the Bend anchor.

"They have no effect on me at all," he claims. "I consider myself a very objective reporter. As a professional I have an obligation to report the news as factually as possible. And as a producer I take very seriously my role as gatekeeper, helping decide what gets on television and what doesn't. Any time there is a story that enlightens people I'll put it on, and I'll do it as objectively as I can."

Ryan recalls only one time when his homosexuality affected his actions in the newsroom. A controversy arose over a local high school support group for gay teens, and a station reporter cited his religious feelings in refusing to cover the story. When the news director allowed the man to bow out, Ryan was upset. "I've done stories where I don't agree with the person I'm interviewing, but I'm a reporter, and I'm objective," he says. His co-anchor was equally furious and felt the reporter should be fired. Ryan talked to his supervisors, but nothing was done. "Management here seldom reprimands people unless it's a huge thing, which I thought this was," he says. "But the news director avoids conflict at all costs. My feeling is, just because you cover something, you don't necessarily endorse it. But they let this guy get away with it. That's not the way a reporter should act."

Gay-related stories pop up infrequently in Bend, but as co-producer of the 11 P.M. news, Ryan tries to include state and national stories when appropriate. He pushed for coverage of the Matthew Shepard murder as well as Portland's gay pride celebrations. Recently, though, he learned there might be more gay stories in town than he realized.

In September 2000 Ryan attended his first NLGJA convention, in San Francisco. Panelists discussed the importance of including gay themes in mainstream stories and of covering often underreported populations such as gay youth. Ryan recalled the earlier high school gay support-group controversy and began planning a story on the importance of the organization for students.

"It's not about any special agenda I have," he insists. "This is a question of shedding light on an important story." He has decided to not frame the piece in traditional, one-side-versus-the-other terms. Because the organization now exists, he says, he will focus on the good they are doing. And he will not seek opinions from the antigay side.

"If I were doing a story on a support group for African-Americans, I wouldn't need to find a spokesman from the Klan to counterbalance it," he says. "The idea is to be sensitive to the concerns and needs of kids and how important this is for them. There are no longer two sides to this story. And I know my news director will not have a problem with it."

Although Ryan feels comfortable in his newsroom and does not consider himself a gay activist, he is a proud member of the gay journalists organization. "As soon as I heard of it I knew I could not *not* join," he says. "I feel very committed to journalism, and anything that helps other journalists come out, that fosters good working environments, and that helps further my profession, I've got to be a part of."

However, he notes, his particular niche—gay television reporters—was tiny. Nearly every print and new media journalist he met asked the same question: "Are you really out in TV?" Yes, he told them, and nearly every other gay TV anchor or weatherman he knows is out too.

"There's an underlying belief that it's hard to be out in television, but I think that's a myth," he says. "Sure, people work very hard to be on TV, no one wants to screw things up, and there's always jockeying to get a better position, but I've never experienced any problems with management, viewers, or sponsors. My own personal life—the personal life of any anchor or reporter—should never enter into what we say or do on air. Our personal life is our own. I'm sure there would be a problem with someone on air promoting a personal agenda, whether it's a gay agenda or a religious one, but I don't think that happens. And simply being gay or following a certain religion when we're off the air is not promoting anything."

Does that mean a television reporter in Victoria, Tex., or Bend, Ore., can someday move up the ranks to bigger markets—Portland, Houston, New York—and wind up in television news's most visible seat, anchoring the network evening news?

"Personally, I don't aspire to be a Tom Brokaw," Ryan says. "But that doesn't mean I haven't thought about how far I can go. I know Peter Jennings is married, but I've never heard anything about his wife. I know if his successor was gay, that would definitely be noted, though. So I think, yes, there is a limit to how far a gay person can go in this business, but that limit is pretty high. There are already openly gay national correspondents and big-city anchors, so who knows what the limit will be?"

Ryan McKeel likes anchoring, but his true love is reporting. His personal goal is to become an investigative reporter on a show like *Dateline NBC* or *20/20*. "Yeah, I'd really like to do that," he says, as if repeating his ambition aloud will bring him closer to it. "In fact, I'm pretty sure there are gay people doing it already."

GINO HORSMAN: DIESEL MECHANIC

A good diesel mechanic possesses certain traits. He must be mechanically inclined, of course—able to take things apart and put them back together. He must also be well organized—not only with the parts he has removed but with tool kits and checklists. And he must be meticulous.

Gino Horsman is a very good diesel mechanic. And, he laughs, part of the reason he is so good is because he is gay. "I'm probably the cleanest, pickiest, most organized mechanic in my whole shop," he says, acknowledging in his Texas twang that a stereotype about gay men (at least in his case) holds true. "I just think there's no excuse for making a mess."

He holds little respect for some of his colleagues at Dallas Area

Rapid Transit, where he maintains buses. "They're not mechanics," he scoffs. "They're parts swappers. I'm pretty good at diagnosing problems. Right from the start I find out what's wrong, and then I fix it. Unfortunately, nowadays these guys just plug the bus in to the computer and start moving parts around until it tells them everything's OK. The way I see it, you gotta love mechanical objects to be a good mechanic."

Gino has loved mechanical objects for as long as he can recall. Through most of his 40 years he has picked things apart—first toys, clocks, and radios, then cars, trucks, and buses—and analyzed their inner workings. For some reason his mother thought he would be a doctor, but the Dallas-area native knew he was too squeamish for that. "Another gay trait," he chuckles.

He bought his first car at the tender age of 12, with proceeds from his lawn mowing business. It was a 1958 BMW Isetta: "A little bubble car I'd never want to be seen driving now." Well under the legal driving age, he terrorized the alleys of suburban Rowlett. When he was not driving his BMW, he was tinkering with it. It was the first of 150 cars he has owned, played with, and sold.

When Gino was 15—and at last old enough to drive legally—his twice-divorced mother could not afford to buy him a good car. Instead she purchased a nice set of mechanic's tools. He taught himself to fix engines, suspensions, and anything else that could go wrong in a vehicle. He kept his sisters' MGs in roadworthy condition and realized he had found a hobby he loved.

In high school he worked with a local mechanic, building race and show cars. Many were featured in automotive magazines. It was a dream job. If that mechanic was still around, Gino says, he would be working with him today.

He was a good student—when he went to school. But the lure of the shop was strong, and he ditched more than his share of classes. College was out of the question. So right after graduation, Gino went to work full-time.

He also discovered racing. He spent his spare time at the Texas Motorplex, a local drag track ("No pun intended!"), and savored the rush of adrenaline he felt every time he slipped behind the wheel. However, even at that level, drag racers must rely on sponsors or private funds. Gino had neither, so after owning a couple of cars he abandoned the sport.

It is the nature of mechanics to move to bigger shops. The lure of better working conditions and more money is strong. Gino did that. For nearly five years he also owned his own towing service.

But mechanics, like everyone else, have private lives and love interests. And in the late '90s Gino met (via the Internet) a man from Virginia named Kenny. Gino, who had come out just a few years earlier, at 31—"I was a late bloomer," he confesses—moved east to be with his new lover. It is nearly impossible to take a Texan out of Texas, however, and today Gino and Kenny live in Garland, where they are building a home. Both work for DART. Kenny, who is less mechanically inclined, is a bus servicer, in charge of checking fluids, cleaning, and gassing. He hopes to move into a clerical position soon.

As a diesel mechanic Gino does "rolling repairs," getting buses back on the street as quickly and safely as possible. It is a fast-paced job but without the pressure of dealerships or service stations, where, he says, "angry customers always need their vehicles right now." He appreciates the responsibility of ensuring the safety of every DART passenger and realizes that each repair he makes must be perfect. The shop he shares with 100 colleagues is fairly laid-back but open 24 hours a day. "The bus line never shuts down, and neither do we," he says proudly.

As much as he enjoys his job—and, he says, DART is "a great organization that promotes from within"—he is not fully himself at work. Gino is not out at DART, and if he can help it, he never plans to be. He lost a previous job, at a BMW dealership, when the manager heard through the grapevine that Gino was gay. Although DART, as a public agency, posts nondiscrimination policies everywhere, Gino also knows that Texas provides no legal protection for gays. "They could fire me and say it was for any ol' reason," he says. So he chooses to say nothing about his private life at work.

"I'm sure people see me and Kenny ride to work together, spend our breaks together, eat lunch together, and they put two and two together," he says. "But I keep remembering the BMW place, where I went from everything being just fine to being the 'faggot' everyone shunned. It's amazing how there can be such a complete turnaround in one day. Evidently people down here have a problem with gay people, and it didn't matter that I was a great mechanic. You've gotta be careful, so I'm just not gonna say anything."

Gino's two trucks sport rainbow flags. However, he notes, "a lot of people in Texas don't know what that is."

Some do, of course. A female bus driver asked Kenny if he and Gino were gay. Kenny told the truth. She, in turn, revealed that her daughter is a lesbian. Gino and the driver became good friends. He often spends the hour before Kenny gets off work talking with her in the break room. She might have told others that the couple is gay, Gino says, but so far no one else has asked him directly.

"The reason I don't tell people 'I am a homosexual' is because I'm there as a mechanic," he explains. "That's my job, and if I choose to keep my private life private, that's my business."

Still, he knows, his friendship with Kenny has raised eyebrows—along with consciousnesses. "Some people ask if we're brothers," he says. "Others have a little more of a clue. One day I was off, and somebody asked Kenny if I'd have dinner waiting when he got home. He said it real nice, though. If someone had the balls to ask straight out, I'd tell him. But I'd still be uncomfortable, due to where I am, saying 'I am a homosexual.' "

Because of their work schedule and the fact that Kenny does not yet know many people in Dallas, the couple's social life is limited. Before he moved to Virginia to be with Kenny, Gino had volunteered as vice president of the Texas Gay Rodeo Association, traveling throughout North America for competitions. He no longer has time to be as active, he says, but may get re-involved in the future.

For now Gino Horsman is happy to share his life with Kenny and relatively content to remain in the closet at the bus shop. "I have to be careful every day," he admits. "I can't call another mechanic 'honey,' and that's the way I talk a lot of the time. But yet, I don't want you to think I'm scared about coming out here. I'm not. It's just...I guess I don't want things to become unpleasant. This is the Southern Bible Belt. There are a lot of bubbas down here. And they carry shotguns in their truck."

DOUG STEVENS:
COUNTRY MUSIC SINGER

Everyone knows that gay men love opera, show tunes, and disco. Gay men do *not* love country music.

Well, hold your horses. That last sentence ain't entirely true. Gay men *do* listen to the twangy guitars, fine fiddles, and bluegrassy dobros that provide heartstring-pulling backup to lyrics about livin', lovin', and all the other good and bad things that happen between birth and death. They listen in Nashville and Austin as well as in country bars in cities coast to coast. Most important, substantial numbers listen in towns and crossroads and flyspecks across the country, joining millions of straight fans young and old to form the foundation of what is arguably America's favorite form of music.

As much as they like country music, however, gay fans, for the most part, do not hear in it reflections of their own lives. The lonesome tears belong to men who love women; the cheatin' hearts to women who sleep with men. Even songs about back roads, hound dogs, and honky-tonk bars have heterosexual subtexts.

Doug Stevens, though, is out to add rainbow hues to country music's all-straight, all-American, red-white-and-blue banner. The 44-year-old singer, founder of the Lesbian and Gay Country Music Association—and, like Elvis Presley, a native of Tupelo, Miss.—is as openly gay as any New York City opera lover, Broadway queen, or Village People fanatic. Who else in the music industry would name his group the Outband or title his first CD *Out in the Country*?

Doug's story, combining hardship and heartache with a healthy dose of sex, sounds like a country music song itself. Born in Tupelo in 1957—the same year Elvis released "All Shook Up" and "Jailhouse Rock"—Doug grew up in a four-room house with no interior doors or indoor plumbing. His family was poor but scraped together enough money to buy guitars. Every night after supper his parents picked and sang. The tunes were mostly old: Jimmie Rodgers classics and songs Doug has never heard since. His mommy and daddy were joined by his "pap-paw" (grandfather), a fiddler, and "mam-maw" (grandmother), who played piano and organ in church and whose brother had a band of his own.

As Doug grew older, his father added rock and roll songs from the '50s to his repertoire of white gospel and traditional country tunes. His kinfolk were "untrained musicians playing out-of-tune instruments," Doug recalls, "but there was just something about it…"

Slowly Doug's father rose up the economic ladder. He moved from extermination work to a factory that manufactured prefabricated houses. At last he struck out on his own, using excellent carpentry skills to build his own homes. Doug and his mother helped. It was a profitable business—at least by Tupelo standards, Doug says—and his father bought a new car and TV. Still, their house lacked a telephone and bathroom.

Eventually the Stevens family moved into a ranch-style home. Doug's parents thought of it as a mansion, but the boy knew it was not. Years of television and movies had helped him soak up main-stream culture, which at that time meant rock music played by the Beatles and Monkees. By adolescence Doug looked down on the country culture he had grown up in. He felt surrounded by alcoholism and spousal abuse; his own father, he says, was physically abusive. He heard older cousins talk about going to college, but they dropped out of high school long before graduation. Doug feared being trapped forever in that dead-end country culture. So at Tupelo High School he studied classical singing. He joined every chorus, earned roles in all the musicals, and even performed operas. He decided his ticket out of Tupelo was as an opera singer.

Doug's father, however, wanted him to stay home and help lay bricks. He refused to pay for his son's college education. Providentially, while Doug was acting in a show the summer after high school, the sister of an actress from St. Louis fell in love with him.

Doug was surprised. Spurred by what little he knew of the nascent gay rights movement, he had come out at 16 to everyone except his parents. He suffered no physical harassment, though his popularity plummeted. (His best friends became two effeminate black chorus members whom everyone assumed were gay. They introduced him to the Red Carpet Lounge in the black section of town, where he had never before ventured. It became his hangout.) Doug told the actress's sister he could never love her the way she wanted him to. She cried, so he tried. They moved to St. Louis together, but he soon realized it was futile to try to be someone he was not.

In Missouri, Doug learned he did not need his father's help; he could pay for college himself. Prodded by Bob Burns, a well educated, emotionally stable, and sophisticated man 17 years his senior whom he had met while singing with the Saint Louis Symphony Chorus, Doug enrolled in Fontbonne College. Bob also encouraged him to major in computer science, not music. After earning his bachelor of science degree, Doug entered the workforce as a computer programmer for McDonnell Douglas.

But he did not like it. He had never lost his love for singing. In fact, he continued singing with the Saint Louis Symphony Chorus, earning money on the side. It was there that he discovered he was not, as he had always believed, a tenor—but rather a countertenor. As he studied recordings of other countertenors who, in his opinion, did not sing well, Doug realized that he could. He began to consider a career in music.

He moved to New York and found work with the Ensemble for Early Music. With these noted performers of medieval and Renaissance works, he toured Europe five times and Hong Kong once. He also found opera work, including a well-paying role with the Cleveland Opera. For five years, Doug says, he "worked like a slave." He studied music, trained his voice, auditioned for jobs, and made sure he did it all superbly.

At the same time he was involved romantically with a dance teacher in Maryland. The two got together whenever they could—holidays, mostly. At the height of the AIDS epidemic, in late 1990, Doug's lover took an HIV test. He was negative. He urged Doug to get tested as well. To both men's surprise and shock, Doug was HIV-positive.

Neither man was emotionally ready for the news; both took it hard. Doug's lover fled, which sent Doug spiraling into depression. He stopped practicing, turned down work, and stayed inside his apartment.

After eight months, however, Doug realized he was not on the verge of death. He told himself to stop being depressed, although he did not know how to do it. One day, sitting in a laundromat in Manhattan's East Village, he suddenly remembered the remedy of fellow Mississippian Tammy Wynette: Whenever she felt depressed she wrote songs.

Doug had never written songs, but suddenly lyrics tumbled out. They were about a lover who left a relationship after learning his partner was HIV-positive.

Though the words came easily, Doug figured the music portion would be much harder. To his amazement, a catchy tune popped into his head. When that song—he called it "HIV Blues"—was done, he wrote another just as quickly. He was astonished at what he could do and stunned that the music that came out of him was country. Equally surprising, he says, was that the country music felt good.

Doug's songwriting explosion in the early '90s coincided with a rise in country music's popularity in urban areas. He had heard of New York gay bars with country music and dancing, deciding to see what they were like. He learned to two-step, and he learned something else too: The same country music he had once derided actually taught lessons about life.

The country bug bit Doug hard. He placed an ad in *The Village Voice* seeking country musicians. It did not take long to form a band—a good one—with a mix of gay, lesbian, and straight members. The Outband got gigs, earned good press, attracted serious investors, and made recordings. Doug formed a second Outband, this one for West Coast tours. The Coors Brewing Co., engaged in an arduous attempt to change its antigay image, signed on as a sponsor.

The mainstream country music world took notice. Writing in the *Journal of Country Music,* a scholarly publication affiliated with the Country Music Hall of Fame and Museum, Chris Dickinson explored with depth and sensitivity Doug's role in the burgeoning gay country music movement. The article paid particular attention to the use of pronoun-specific lyrics. "Instead of 'she' or the ambiguous 'you,' " Dickinson wrote, Doug makes it "perfectly clear that his love songs are specifically about men, not women. Combining raucous and raw honky-tonk stylings with occasional forays into more pop-influenced contemporary country, Stevens's songs tackle the joys and heartbreaks of gay relationships."

Dickinson cited "the sad, loping 'Living a Lie in Georgia,' a wounding meditation on a lesbian hitting the road out of her small hometown after her secret is revealed." The lyrics, he noted, "are open enough for universal interpretation. On one level it's a song that will resonate with anyone whose otherness creates rupture with home and family, a paean to the displacement and emotional isolation that one finds in so many Merle Haggard songs." However, Dickinson continued, "listened to from a gay perspective, it nails the often traumatic consequences that go hand in hand with coming out, the community and familial ostracism one risks in being honest about sexual preference."

Doug's songs cover a broad swath of gay life. "Out in the Country," the title tune from his debut CD of the same name, is about his cousin—the boy who taught him all about romance and manly pleasures. "Git While the Gittin's Good" describes the temptations of a sexy man at a bar while a sweet lover waits back home. "ACT UP" is an angry song excoriating two Republican administrations' inaction during the AIDS crisis.

Doug's second CD, *When Love Is Right,* includes "Proud to Be an American," the true story of a blond 6-foot-4 ex-marine who could die for his country but was not allowed to love; "Pump-n-Go," inspired by hot gas station attendants; "Daisy," about a transvestite Doug knew back at Tupelo's Red Carpet Lounge, and "Hang Your Clothes in the Closet (and Wear Yourself With Pride)," an anthem encouraging gay people to come out wherever they are.

His third CD, *From Christopher to Castro,* will be released soon. It too will contain a number of songs about relationships. "As gay people we're told so often that our love is wrong or bad, that we're promiscuous or nasty," Doug explains. "Even after therapy a lot of negativity remains. Through my songs I try to show that we can have lives filled with goodness, honor, and innocence."

In 1998, no longer content simply singing and playing, Doug formed the Lesbian and Gay Country Music Association. The organization's mission is clearly stated on its Web site: to "promote and encourage lesbian and gay singers, musicians, and songwriters who write and perform country music." But the *Journal of Country Music's* Chris Dickinson described it more fully: "At the heart of the LGCMA beats one common belief: that the emotional core of country music— with its evocative emphasis on loss, heartbreak, and the healing possibilities of love—belongs to anyone who finds comfort and expression in it. The organization is not politically militant. Instead it serves as a gesture of support, a lifting of the head above the trenches into visibility, a way of embracing country as a music that, despite backward stereotypes, emotionally cuts across age, race, and sexual preference lines."

Of course, not all of that embrace sits easily with the country music establishment. When Doug told The Nashville Network's *Country News* segment the exciting news that the Book-of-the-Month Club was finally selling country recordings—and that it all started with *Out in the Country*—the preeminent country channel told him they could no longer say the word "gay" on air. Apparently an earlier mention of country music's popularity with gay listeners had unleashed a torrent of hate mail.

Doug also says that the Bluebird Cafe, one of Nashville's premier performance spots, reneged on an invitation after someone there realized exactly what kind of music the Outband played.

But those are minor bumps on the country road. Year after year, through dogged guerrilla marketing, sheer persistence, and relentlessly high-energy, upbeat performances at pride festivals, fund-raisers, dances, college campuses—even gay rodeos—Doug spreads two important messages: Country music is not just for straight people, and it's OK for gay folks to love it too.

"When you drive across America, it's very clear this is the most popular music," he says with conviction. "Gays and lesbians are a substantial part of that American population, even outside the coasts." At the same time, however, substantial discrimination exists against country culture. As Doug explains, "It's not urban or exciting. Well, urban culture can be dehumanizing and alienating. Country music is exactly what it seems: a narrative story that takes you on an emotional trip. I think whether you're gay or straight, when you reach a certain age you don't want alienation—you want to connect with other people. Country music helps you do that, whoever you are."

When Doug first formed the Outband, his goal was to play for straight audiences as well as gay. However, a recording executive advised him to saturate his own community first. As a result he has stuck—happily—with a gay fan base. Fortunately, there are plenty of gay fans, and he has discovered, to his delight, they love what he does. At San Francisco Pride, concertgoers showered Doug and the band with flowers. Gay men packed a bar for an AIDS service organization fund-raiser in Mobile, Ala., standing on tables and screaming with

delight at the chance to hear what Doug describes as "our masculine, kick-ass music."

But even if he does not play kick-ass music in front of straight fans, Nashville's cognoscenti know Doug. At a gay business exhibition in New York, Merle Haggard's nephew introduced himself, then delightedly described how Doug's CD had been played at the country superstar's recent birthday party.

At one time news like that might have thrilled Doug. Now, he says, he does not really care. His aim is not to be the next Randy Travis. Today, he has two main purposes in life. One is to use his artistic talents to help members of the gay and lesbian community feel good about themselves; the other is to send a message that gay men and lesbians really are everywhere.